To Sara,
     May this book help you grow
closer to Jesus!
               Love,
          Tíos Mike y Ma. Elena.
                              Dic/21.

# GROW IN GRACE

## 5-MINUTE DEVOTIONS FOR PRETEEN GIRLS

Megan Gover

Illustrations by TheLittleLabs Studio

ROCKRIDGE PRESS

Interior and Cover Designer: Angie Chiu
Art Producer: Samantha Ulban
Editor: Erum Khan
Associate Editor: Maxine Marshall
Production Editor: Jenna Dutton

Illustrations © 2020 TheLittleLabs Studio
Author photo courtesy of © The Tarnos Photography

ISBN: Print 978-1-64739-695-4 | eBook 978-1-64739-696-1

R0

# INTRODUCTION

**Right now, it probably feels like everything in your life is changing.** You're probably getting ready to switch schools or adjust to harder classes. Your body may be developing, and you might feel excited or nervous (or both!) about it. Maybe you're making new friends through sports teams or extracurricular activities. Even the way you hang out with your friends on a Saturday afternoon is probably different than it was a year ago. All that change can feel fun, but it can also feel really overwhelming.

Because you're living through so much change, you probably have a million questions that all seem like they need to be answered right now. Questions about your dreams for the future and mistakes you've made in the past. Questions about how you can help your family, trust your friends, and feel confident every day. The good news is, everyone has these questions. But it can be really hard to figure out the answers on your own.

Luckily, you don't have to figure life out by yourself. God gave us the Bible so that we can learn from Him and feel His support, instead of feeling like we have to live life all alone. You'll go through all different kinds of growth and change in the next few years. But developing your relationship with Jesus is some of the most important growth you'll ever experience. I found this to be true in my own life.

When I was a little girl, I saw my parents and grandparents grow in their love and relationship with Jesus as they studied the Bible. I would often wake up to find an open Bible on the kitchen table, a sign of their early morning time with the Lord. For my parents and grandparents, studying Scripture wasn't just a habit; the Bible was a treasure for them. It taught them the love of Christ and transformed them to live more like Him.

As I entered my teen years, I desperately wanted to have a relationship like this with Jesus, so I started to seriously study the Bible through daily reading. God revealed something new to me about His character as I spent time with Him. He showed me the power of His love, kindness, and compassion. I learned how to serve my neighbor and exhibit the fruits of the Spirit. I went to the Lord with my every need, desire, and fear. I wasn't studying God's Word because I felt I had to. I began to crave spending time with the Lord because I wanted to. The truth found in the Bible has forever changed me. And it has the power to change you, too.

Throughout this book, we will be studying Scripture together. Each page includes a Bible verse that will help you learn more about God and how He can help you navigate middle school, friendships, and more. At the end of every devotion, there is space for you to jot down notes, thoughts, questions, and prayers.

Each devotion should only take about five minutes, so you can read it at any time of day. You might choose to start your day by reading a devotion while eating breakfast, or it might be the perfect thing to think about right before your head hits the pillow at night. Choose a routine that works for you and stick with it. And if you like, invite an adult to explore the devotions with you. You might enjoy sharing your thoughts with someone important in your life.

Whether you've already spent a lot of time studying the Bible or this is all new to you, spending time in God's Word will help you grow into a girl of grace. I can't wait to join you on this journey. My prayer is that this book sparks a lifetime of learning and loving God. May the Lord become your greatest treasure as you continue to seek Him!

# CELEBRATING GOD'S LOVE

*For God so loved the world that He gave His one and only Son,*
*that whoever believes in Him shall not perish but have eternal life.*

JOHN 3:16

What's the best gift you've ever received? Maybe when you were little, there was a toy you couldn't stop thinking about—and then you found it under the tree on Christmas morning. Or maybe your friends surprised you with all your favorite snacks on your birthday. Gifts from the people we love make us feel appreciated.

But the gift of God's love is different from any gift you've received before. In John 3:16, one of Jesus's disciples described this gift. John declared that God loved the world so much that He sent His Son, Jesus, to die on the Cross. This gift made it so that anyone who believes in God is forgiven of their sins and can have a relationship with Him—both in this life and the next. This gift of God's forgiveness is not something that we have to work for; Jesus gives it to us out of love. All we have to do is accept it.

When you receive a present, what do you usually do? First, you thank the giver. Then, you just can't help but tell others about your new gift. You can respond in the same way to the gift of God's love. When you pray or study the Bible, you thank God for loving you. And when you are kind to others, you share this gift with the people around you.

God's gift of forgiveness and love is the greatest gift we could ever receive. We should celebrate it!

REFLECT

What actions can you take to thank God for His boundless love? How can you share that love with the people around you?

5

# THE AMAZING STORY OF THE GOSPEL

When you think about your favorite stories, what qualities do they all have in common? They probably have excitement, action, and adventure. The Gospel has all of that and more. It is the life-and-death story of Christ's love for us, and it goes all the way back to creation, when Adam and Eve sinned in the Garden of Eden. They had a perfect relationship with God until Satan talked them into eating fruit that the Lord had forbidden them to eat. Their actions introduced sin to the world.

God is holy, which means that He cannot have sin in His presence. But, because He loves us, God made a plan to redeem the world. The Lord sent His one and only Son, Jesus, to pay the price for our sins. Jesus died on the Cross, and then, three days later, He rose from the dead. Jesus, therefore, has victory over sin and death. This truth is the heart of the Gospel.

If you want to accept God's love and salvation, it's simple. The Bible says you must admit you have sinned, believe Jesus died on the Cross for your sins, and declare He is the Lord. Accepting the truth of the Gospel allows you to have a relationship with God today and every day.

Jesus offers forgiveness to all who ask for it. Turn to Him for love and mercy.

REFLECT

What do you think is the best part of the story of the Gospel? Who can you share the good news of the Gospel with today?

# CLOTHING YOURSELF IN KINDNESS

Therefore, as God's chosen people, holy and dearly loved,
clothe yourselves with compassion, kindness,
humility, gentleness, and patience.

COLOSSIANS 3:12

You'd think that figuring out what to wear every morning would be simple. After all, you only have so many items of clothing! Picking an outfit can be difficult, but in the end you have to decide on something.

Just like we choose our outfits, we must also choose to clothe ourselves in kindness. This should be a basic part of your routine, just like getting dressed.

Throughout the Bible, everything God does is rooted in kindness. When we had no hope, Jesus brought hope to the world. Kindness is the basis of the love He shows us every day. Since we receive the Lord's constant grace, we should extend the same loving goodness to others.

Acts of kindness don't have to be big—every time you are nice to someone, you share the love that God has given you. When you offer your classmate your last piece of candy or forgive your sibling, you share God's kindness.

We can never repay God for all the ways we benefit from His loving compassion, but the way we choose to live demonstrates our gratitude. So, after you decide on your outfit, don't forget to choose kindness, too!

REFLECT
Have you ever felt encouraged by someone's kindness?

# SHOWING EMPATHY

*Rejoice with those who rejoice; mourn with those who mourn.*
ROMANS 12:15

Sympathy is showing someone that you understand how they're feeling, like when you congratulate a friend for winning a soccer game.

Empathy goes even deeper than sympathy. When we experience empathy, we don't just understand someone's emotions; we actually feel them, too.

In the New Testament, Paul reminded the Roman church to show their love through action. He said they could do this by rejoicing when others rejoice and mourning when others mourn. Paul asked the members of the church to feel other people's emotions deeply.

Empathy allows us to relate to others by placing ourselves in their shoes. Showing compassion to someone who is mourning helps you imagine the heartache they feel. Instead of trying to fix their problems, you can understand their sadness and offer comfort.

Empathy is also about participating in other people's joy. Imagine that you have a friend who is nervous about her social studies test, so she studies hard for days. When she gets her test back and sees that she got an A, empathy calls for sharing her joy. Celebrate others by responding to their joy the way you would want them to respond to yours.

When our feelings match the feelings of those around us, people know they are not alone in whatever situation they are facing.

REFLECT
Has anyone ever shown you empathy?

_____

_____

_____

# GROWING CLOSER TO GOD

*Come near to God and He will come near to you.*

JAMES 4:8

As you meet new people, have new experiences, and grow older, many things in your life will change. But one truth is constant: we are as close to God as we choose to be.

If you feel distant from God, odds are you are either lacking in desire or discipline. Maybe you would rather turn on the TV than open the Bible because you're tired. And it's easy to get caught up in the routines of school and sports. But just as you make time to grow as a student or athlete, you must also intentionally carve out time to grow as a follower of Jesus.

Perhaps you struggle with regret over past mistakes, and you feel like you don't deserve God's grace. Instead of running to the Lord, you might run away from Him because you feel you've messed up too much. Ultimately, your discipline and desire work together to remove the roadblocks in your heart and habits that keep you from developing a deeper relationship with Jesus.

If you want to be closer to God, the first step is to admit your sins and mistakes. Confessing any wrongdoing to the Lord opens the door for Christ's forgiveness. When you are reminded that you are loved and forgiven, it becomes much easier to seek God.

You don't have to play games or pretend to be someone you're not to feel closer to God. To cultivate a relationship with Jesus, all you have to do is accept His invitation for forgiveness.

REFLECT

Do you have any roadblocks that sometimes keep you from feeling close to Jesus?

# LOVING YOUR BODY

*For you created my inmost being; you knit me together in my mother's womb. I praise you because I am fearfully and wonderfully made; your works are wonderful, I know that full well.*

**PSALM 139:13–14**

No matter who you ask—your friends, your family, even celebrities— you'll find that everyone struggles with feeling good about their body at times. Some days, you might be proud of how strong you feel pirouetting in your ballet class or happy about how your smile looks in a photo. Other times, you might be embarrassed by a zit that popped up on your chin or wish you looked more like the actors on TV.

Though we all go through these ups and downs, it is important to remember that God gave us our bodies with a single purpose: to glorify Him. We can worship God by celebrating the miracle of our living bodies.

Our heart, lungs, brain, and muscles perform complicated and amazing jobs. And not only did God create us to be so intricate—He created us intentionally, too. From the beginning of time, God knew your hair color, your skin tone, and which parent's nose you would get. He lovingly dreamt you up and has given each of us His stamp of approval. All of these miracles and mysteries should stir our hearts to worship God because of His great power and creativity.

The next time you look in the mirror, don't focus on things you don't like. Instead, try thinking about the ways God has made you wonderful.

REFLECT

What aspects of your body do you often find yourself criticizing? How does knowing that God is our Creator help you love your body better?

# REJOICING ALWAYS

Rejoice in the Lord always. I will say it again: Rejoice!

PHILIPPIANS 4:4

Happiness and joy sound interchangeable, but they are actually very different. Happiness is a response to the things happening around you. Joy is a deep-seated attitude that comes from your delight in God, separate from your circumstances. We can have joy in moments of happiness and in seasons of sadness. This doesn't mean you are happy about your disappointment. Joy is anchored in God and your trust that He is in control of your life, regardless of what happens.

The apostle Paul knew this better than anyone. When he wrote the book of Philippians, he was in jail, where he had been imprisoned because of his faith. As you can imagine, this was not an easy place for Paul to feel happy, but joy anchored Paul's attitude. When his situation was rocky, he used his faith to find joy in an unshakable God.

Not only was Paul filled with joy, but he instructed other believers to find joy, too. Notice when he said to rejoice: *always*. When you are happy about the grade you got on a test? Thank the Lord! When your parents talk about getting a divorce? Rejoice and be grateful that God is close to you in your pain. Rejoicing isn't a suggestion but a comforting command to trust God when you face hard circumstances. There is always something to enjoy about God.

When we rejoice, we trust God's understanding of our lives. He knows our hearts, needs, and desires and is faithful until the end.

REFLECT
How would you describe the difference between joy and happiness?

# BENEFITING FROM GOD'S WORD

*All Scripture is God-breathed and is useful for teaching, rebuking, correcting, and training in righteousness, so that the servant of God may be thoroughly equipped for every good work.*

**2 TIMOTHY 3:16–17**

*Scripture* and *God's Word* are just two of the many names we have for the Bible. Although it might be easy to think that the Bible is just a book, we know that Scripture is a living, active record of God's love for us (Hebrews 4:12–13). Each page is filled with the breath of God, sharing His truth and life.

God's Word lays the foundation for our actions. It teaches us about sin and God's forgiveness. It calls us out when we make mistakes, gently corrects us, and teaches us how to live righteously. Though the Bible refreshes our souls, makes us wise, and gives us joy, it's not always necessarily enjoyable realizing the ways we mess up. But studying the Bible helps us live more like Christ.

When we find that we're not spending time with God's Word, we might feel guilty or ashamed. But there's no need to feel that. Instead, let the benefits of Scripture invite you to know Jesus better. Reading Scripture is not something we *have* to do—it's the greatest thing we *get* to do.

**REFLECT**

Why is it important for the Bible to teach, correct, and train us? If there is great benefit in reading God's Word, what holds you back from studying it?

# SHARING GOD'S LOVE ON SOCIAL MEDIA

*Follow God's example, therefore, as dearly loved children and walk in the way of love, just as Christ loved us and gave Himself up for us.*

EPHESIANS 5:1–2

Have you ever copied someone you looked up to? Maybe when you were little, you wanted to dress the same as your big sister. Or perhaps you're looking forward to joining the same club your mom did in high school. We often copy our heroes because we feel close to them and want to be more like them. This also applies to our relationship with God. As we grow closer to the Lord, we show Christ's love to others by acting as He did.

One way you can mirror the Lord's love is on social media. Most of us use social media to talk to our friends and share interesting details about our lives. There's nothing wrong with any of that. However, if you begin to base your confidence on how many likes you get, you might start posting things that lack integrity, like inappropriate pictures or gossip.

Instead of using social media to build up your own reputation, share the Lord's goodness on it. Consider commenting on a friend's post with a thoughtful compliment. Or DM some words of encouragement to someone who seems sad. Anytime you create a post that shares love and positivity, you help share God's kindness.

The next time you log on, allow the Lord's love to guide how you interact with friends and followers.

REFLECT

Have you seen other people use social media to encourage others? How can you use social media to reflect God's love?

_____

_____

_____

# HANDLING YOUR ANGER

"In your anger do not sin": Do not let the sun go down while you are
still angry, and do not give the devil a foothold.

EPHESIANS 4:26-27

We've all felt anger. Some forms of anger can be destructive, especially anger about personal concerns. This kind of anger can lead
us to act aggressively and do things like speak disrespectfully to a
parent or ignore a friend. We become focused only on our needs,
blinded by selfishness. When we allow anger to come between us
and the people we love, Satan wins by dividing us.

However, as Paul instructed Christ's followers in the book of
Ephesians, the emotion of anger is not always sinful. Even Jesus
got angry!

Throughout the New Testament, when people disrespected God
or mistreated others, Christ responded with anger. But when He
was angry, Jesus never acted cruelly. Instead, He expressed Himself
and worked to correct the situation.

Anger serves a purpose when it is expressed in a safe and reason-
able way. It motivates us to act on our love for God and speak up
when we see something that is wrong. When you feel irritated by a
bully's abuse of your classmates or distressed about poverty, you are
mirroring the Lord's holiness. Being outraged by the same things
that outrage God encourages us to stand up for what is right.

If you find yourself battling anger, give yourself some time and
space to work through your emotions. Ask yourself what's making
you angry. Then, ask the Lord to help you reflect Christ's character
by getting angered by the things that anger Him.

REFLECT
What makes you angry? How do you express that anger?

# RESISTING PEER PRESSURE

*Do not conform to the pattern of this world, but be transformed by the renewing of your mind. Then you will be able to test and approve what God's will is—His good, pleasing, and perfect will.*

**ROMANS 12:2**

When you experience peer pressure, you consider making a choice that you normally wouldn't because you think it will help you fit in.

This desire to fit in isn't new. Thousands of years ago, members of the early Roman church were tempted to change their beliefs so that other people would accept them. Paul responded by reminding them that they were not to be shaped by the world's desires. Instead, he reminded the members of the church about God's commandments.

When you feel peer pressure, pause to remember Scripture. It will remind you that you don't have to act like someone else in order to belong, because you already belong to Christ.

Just because standing up to peer pressure is right doesn't mean that it's easy. But remember that God is there to support you when you push back against peer pressure. So are your family members and your true friends.

When you are pressured to do something that doesn't feel right, step away from the situation for a moment to restore your heart. Don't be afraid to ask God or someone you trust for advice.

**REFLECT**

Have you experienced peer pressure? Write down truths about God's love that you can think about the next time you are feeling pressured.

_____

_____

_____

# CALMING YOUR WORRIES

*Therefore do not worry about tomorrow, for tomorrow will worry about itself. Each day has enough trouble of its own.*

MATTHEW 6:34

What makes you feel worried? Taking tests? Thinking about your family's money struggles? When we worry, we fear for the future. Sometimes, the problems that you worry about can be handled with the right amount of preparation. If you're worried about a test, for example, you can make sure to study. But other problems are bigger than we can control. Either way, God offers us comfort and a solution. Instead of spending time and energy worrying about things that are out of our control, we can trust the Lord, who is in control of it all.

When we sweat the small stuff, like food choices or outfit options, we forget that God provides for everything in creation, like birds and flowers, and for us, too. Worrying can show a lack of trust in God's capacity to provide. But the God who created Earth doesn't forget to take care of His creation.

In Matthew 6:34, Jesus commanded His disciples not to fear for the future because God knows exactly what we need. We can enjoy today instead of worrying about tomorrow, because worry does not add anything valuable to our lives.

When worry starts to whisper, turn to the Lord in worship. Understanding the Lord's desire to provide for you can calm your worry and help you plan for your next step.

### REFLECT
Jot down some of the Lord's qualities. How can these characteristics help you worry less?

---

---

---

# TRUSTING GOD

*Trust in the Lord with all your heart and lean not on your own understanding; in all your ways submit to Him, and He will make your paths straight.*

PROVERBS 3:5–6

We can rely on the Lord in all areas of our lives. He is unchanging and constant. We can trust the Lord because nothing is too powerful for Him to conquer or too small for Him to notice. We can put our hope in God's strength, for it will never fail. Instead of relying on our limited understanding of situations, we can place our trust in God's guidance.

King Solomon was a wise and wealthy man. If anyone could feel confident in their riches, kingdom, or power, it would have been him. Yet even King Solomon realized that God should be the sole source of his trust. King Solomon knew God was more reliable than anything else in his life.

Overall, God knows what's best for us. The habit of trusting in God's wisdom eliminates our daily worries. You can feel secure knowing that the Lord knows every emotion in your heart. When you feel tired, confused, or powerless, it can be comforting to remind yourself that God is in control even when you are not.

The next time you try to lean on your own understanding, remind yourself of King Solomon, who taught us that God is more reliable than money or power. God will continue to be there to support you, even if everything else in your life changes.

REFLECT
Why can you trust God? How can you act on that trust to guide your decisions?

*For we are God's handiwork, created in Christ Jesus to do good works, which God prepared in advance for us to do.*

EPHESIANS 2:10

When we admire the beauty of nature, we recognize God as Creator. The depths of the Grand Canyon and the enormity of the ocean show His power and creativity. But out of all the natural wonders of the world, God considers humanity His best creation.

This truth means God handpicked every quality that makes you *you*. The Lord placed every star in the sky and every freckle on your face. From the inside out, we've been uniquely created by God. But it can be easy to forget all of our own wonderful qualities when we compare ourselves to others. Unfortunately, when you forget to find joy in the gifts that God has given you, it is much harder to use those gifts.

When Paul wrote to the Ephesian church, he reminded believers that their physical and spiritual lives were gifts from God. The best way to thank the Lord for these gifts is to make use of the way that He wired us.

The Lord gave some of us shy personalities to represent His gentleness in the world. Others display His joy through outgoing personalities. Some of us have strong leadership skills, while others bring peace to chaotic situations. Instead of believing our unique qualities are random quirks, we can take joy in knowing that God made each of us the way we are for a reason. We glorify the Lord when we use our unique gifts.

REFLECT

What are some of your unique qualities?

# FACING EMBARRASSMENT

*A cheerful heart is good medicine,*
*but a crushed spirit dries up the bones.*

PROVERBS 17:22

When was the last time you felt embarrassed? Maybe you left the restroom without noticing that a piece of toilet paper was stuck to your shoe. Whatever it was, it was probably tough. Embarrassment is one of the worst feelings, and it can make us feel really uncomfortable and unsettled.

When we are embarrassed, it is usually because we are worried about what others think of us. The book of Proverbs has wisdom for all types of circumstances, including feeling embarrassed.

The Bible declares that a cheerful heart is medicine for a crushed spirit. We can choose to lighten an awkward situation by changing our response to embarrassing moments. If you accidentally walk into school with your shirt inside out, humor and a cheerful heart can bring perspective to the situation.

In moments where you find yourself feeling awkward or uncomfortable, lift your heart by laughing at yourself. We all have embarrassing moments, but we get to choose how we handle them. So, let's embrace the odd situations we find ourselves in with a cheerful heart. Life is more enjoyable when we are laughing.

REFLECT
What is one of your most embarrassing stories? How did humor help keep you from getting discouraged? Or how could humor have helped this situation?

# BUILDING A HABIT OF PRAYER

*Rejoice always, pray continually, give thanks in all circumstances;
for this is God's will for you in Christ Jesus.*

1 THESSALONIANS 5:16–18

Your phone is essential because it connects you to loved ones. Whether you're using it to text a friend, call your grandma, or check social media, your phone helps you stay in touch. Prayer is like a spiritual phone—it helps us communicate with God. And we should use it as often as we use our real phones.

You might not pray as often because you feel stumped about how to pray and what to pray for. Luckily, Jesus offered His disciples the Lord's Prayer as a template. In this example prayer, Jesus covered everything from praising God to asking for daily food to resisting temptation when it arises. When you aren't sure how to pray or what to include, turn to Jesus's example for guidance.

We don't have to set aside special time or do any special ceremony in order to pray. Prayer is a conversation with the Lord, and He's available to listen 24/7.

Although God is always available, we sometimes forget to pray, so we must continually remind ourselves. Choose something in your life that can help you remember to communicate with God. Maybe every time a bell rings at school, you can take a few seconds to pray before your next class. Or every time you touch your phone, say a prayer before you use it.

The Lord promises He will always hear our prayers, so why not pray more often?

REFLECT

What are some ways you can remind yourself to pray during the day?

# LEADING BY EXAMPLE

Don't let anyone look down on you because you are young,
but set an example for the believers in speech,
in conduct, in love, in faith, and in purity.

1 TIMOTHY 4:12

When you are young, it's easy to feel like you can't make an impact on the world. You might feel like you don't have enough experience, talent, or resources to make a difference. However, as a young follower of Jesus, you have the power to set an example and to encourage others to follow Him, too.

In the Bible, the apostle Paul mentored a young pastor named Timothy. Older adults discouraged Timothy from leading their church because they thought he was too young. But Paul gently reminded Timothy that the only thing required to set an example for others is having a genuine relationship with Jesus.

The way we live our lives is a statement of God's love in our hearts. Under God's influence, our words and our actions are thoughtful. When we honor the Lord in our lives, our relationships and motives are rooted in love.

When we joyfully seek Jesus, God's love becomes contagious to those around us. When older believers see young people like you following Jesus, it encourages them. Our relationship with Jesus can be equally inspiring for friends or younger believers. So, don't worry that you don't have enough power or influence to change anything. Instead, set an example of how to follow Christ.

REFLECT
When did you set a good example?

# FORGIVING OTHERS

Bear with each other and forgive one another if any of you has
a grievance against someone. Forgive as the Lord forgave you.

**COLOSSIANS 3:13**

Asking for forgiveness is difficult. It's hard to admit that you were
wrong and that you hurt somebody you love. But forgiving someone else can be just as difficult. Sometimes, you might want to hold
a grudge instead of letting someone apologize. When someone
hurts you, you have a choice: you can stay hurt, or you can forgive
others as Christ forgave us all.

One of the ways the Lord transforms our hearts is through His
forgiveness. Forgiveness is a choice to love people instead of hold-
ing their actions against them. When Paul offered the Colossian
church instructions about how to live with Christ's love in their
lives, he told them to forgive each other as the Lord forgave them.

If it is difficult for you to forgive others, take a moment to remind
yourself how God loves and forgives you. He doesn't keep a list of all
your mistakes to use against you later. Every time we mess up, we
get a fresh start because Christ forgave all our sins when He died on
the Cross. So, we can all follow His example by offering forgiveness
to each other. When a friend says something mean, remember the
countless times the Lord has forgiven the cruel things you've said
to others. If a sibling does something hurtful, think of the times you
accidentally hurt a loved one.

Choose to be generous with your forgiveness. Give others the
grace you've received from Christ.

REFLECT
How do you usually respond when someone hurts you?

_____

_____

_____

# HONORING THE LORD WITH YOUR BODY

*Do you not know that your bodies are temples of the Holy Spirit, who is in you, whom you have received from God? You are not your own; you were bought at a price. Therefore honor God with your bodies.*

1 CORINTHIANS 6:19–20

It can be challenging to see our bodies as blessings. You might look in the mirror and wish you looked different. Or you might feel annoyed at all the work to keep your braces clean. But instead of feeling frustrated, you can choose to feel grateful for the body God gave you. In fact, treating your body wisely and with love is a wonderful way to honor the Lord.

When the apostle Paul wrote to the Corinthian church, he reminded believers that the Holy Spirit lives within us, and he described our bodies as temples. This means that your body is a holy gift, and you should care for it thoughtfully. You might wish you could eat pizza every night instead of a healthy dinner. You might hate brushing your teeth. But we keep our bodies healthy to honor God, whose Holy Spirit lives inside us.

Though living healthily is a way to worship the Lord, our bodies also serve a spiritual purpose. We honor the Lord when we use our bodies for holiness rather than for sinful desires. When you have a crush or crave a tub of ice cream, temptations can make it seem like you should use your body however feels best in the moment. But Paul made it clear: We must use our bodies in a way that honors God. When you treat your body as the holy temple it is, it is an act of worship.

REFLECT
How can you treat your body like a temple?

_____

_____

_____

# LEARNING FROM BAD DECISIONS

*The prudent see danger and take refuge,*
*but the simple keep going and pay the penalty.*

PROVERBS 27:12

When was the last time you made a bad decision? Maybe you needed to study, but decided not to. Or perhaps you spoke rudely about someone behind their back. We all mess up; it's a fact of life. It is also a fact that, no matter whether the bad decision you make is big or small, there are always consequences.

Proverbs, a book in the Bible about practical tips for living, teaches us about wisdom. Wisdom, or prudence, helps us see danger coming so we can make the right decision about how to handle it. According to Proverbs, those who are wise see potential danger and turn away from it. But those who see danger and continue heading toward it pay the penalty.

Learning from our past bad decisions illuminates the dangers of going down the same path again. Our mistakes teach us how to live wisely.

When you need to make a decision, you have two options. You can choose to be wise, think things through, and act in a way that won't create negative consequences. Or you can choose to repeat your past bad decisions and pay the price for them again. Choosing wisely leads you to freedom. Choosing poorly traps you in a pattern of bad decisions and consequences.

REFLECT

What is a bad decision that you made recently? How might you act differently in the future?

# FEELING LONELY

*Never will I leave you; never will I forsake you.*

HEBREWS 13:5

When you can't connect with friends at school or feel distant from family members, it can make you feel alone. When your friends, family members, or teachers don't make time for you, it's because they are busy or distracted, not because they don't care about you. But even though they don't do it on purpose, you may still feel let down.

Luckily, when we feel left out and sad, a quick cure is to remind ourselves that Christ is always near. God chooses to always be with us. He never gets too busy or distracted. In both the Old and New Testaments, God promises He will never leave us. In fact, Jesus is called *Immanuel*, which means "God with us." He will never ditch us. He truly is the perfect friend in moments of loneliness.

Know that sometimes loneliness is a result of anxiety or depression. If you can't shake the feeling of isolation, reach out to a trusted adult.

When you realize you are not alone in this world, you can also recognize the joy of comforting others in their loneliness. Odds are, others around you feel incredibly lonely, too. Instead of waiting for someone to reach out to you, make a brave move to help others with their loneliness. If a classmate has seemed discouraged recently, invite them to sit with you at lunch. Or make time to hang out with a sibling who is having problems with friends. You may never know how your actions encourage others.

REFLECT

When have you felt lonely? Take a moment to consider God's promise to never leave you. How does that make you feel?

_____

_____

_____

25

# FINDING COMFORT IN CHRIST

*Praise be to the God and Father of our Lord Jesus Christ,
the Father of compassion and the God of all comfort,
who comforts us in all our troubles, so that we can comfort those
in any trouble with the comfort we ourselves receive from God.*

**2 CORINTHIANS 1:3–4**

There are probably a lot of different things that help calm your worries and fears, like a hug from your mom or a plate of your grandma's macaroni and cheese. Though these things might comfort you, nothing compares to the comfort we receive from Christ.

When life is tough, God helps us work through our sadness. God is the Father of all compassion and the God of all comfort. This means that He strengthens us when we are tired. This encouragement might come in the form of wise words from a youth leader or from a Bible verse that matches the feelings we are experiencing. God chooses to comfort us in many ways.

The apostle Paul knew a lot about God's comfort. Throughout his ministry, Paul went to jail and faced many other hard situations. He felt despair. But he focused on God's comfort during discouraging times and offered advice so that others could do the same.

God always gives us comfort, but He also asks us to share it with others. Maybe a Bible verse that helped you through a difficult time can help a friend going through a similar struggle. If a youth leader's advice gave you hope, you might want to pass it on to a classmate. Allow the comfort you receive from God to give strength to those around you.

REFLECT
Think of a time when God gave you comfort. How are you using this comfort to encourage your friends and family?

_____

_____

_____

# LIVING A LIFE OF PURITY

*How can a young person stay on the path of purity?*
*By living according to your word.*

**PSALM 119:9**

Do you know about water filters? They remove dirt and impurities from our water, cleaning it so that we can safely drink it. Similarly, God's Word acts as a filter in our lives, helping identify sin and wrongdoing so that our hearts can be pure.

Many people think differently than we, as believers, do about what kinds of actions are right and good. Sometimes, when we see other people use crass language or take part in risky behavior, it looks easy and exciting. To understand what is good, we must be careful to follow the Word of God to guide our decisions.

Scripture is the living Word of God. It shows us what is good and helps us to see areas where we might need to change. But if we want to do the right thing, we can't just read or listen to God's Word. We must also live according to God's instructions.

For example, reading the commandment to love your neighbor might help you realize that you're angry at a classmate. But just knowing that isn't enough. You also need to take action. Going above and beyond to show this person kindness is what will purify your heart and bring you closer to God.

Living according to God's Word aligns us with His desire for us to have clean hearts. Allow God's Word to be a filter on your heart, mind, and soul, and you'll stay on the path of purity.

**REFLECT**
What temptations are the strongest for you? Write down a Bible verse that can help you filter out those temptations.

# WITNESSING BULLYING

*Love your neighbor as yourself.*

**LUKE 10:27**

You've probably witnessed bullying at your school. Maybe you've seen an eighth grader knock the books out of a sixth grader's hands. Maybe you've seen classmates tease someone about the way they dress. Maybe these things, or others, have happened to you. Bullying comes in many different forms. But the love of Jesus demands that we stand up against all of it.

Luckily, Jesus gave us an example of how to love our neighbors in the parable of the Good Samaritan. He told the story of a man who was robbed and left injured on the side of the road. Three people walked by, but only the Samaritan helped, cleaning the man up and paying for a place for him to stay.

This parable makes it clear: if someone is being bullied, our most loving action is to help them or to stop the bully. We cannot say we love our neighbors and then stand by while they suffer. We cannot say we love someone and then bully or hurt them. The love we receive from Jesus encourages us to love others and use our gifts to help them.

Think about tangible ways to show love the next time you see someone being bullied. You might actively step in to stop the bully, get a teacher or parent involved, or offer encouragement after the event is over. Regardless, Christ's example should be your guide. Today, let's seek out those who are hurt and love them just as Christ loves us.

REFLECT

If you were being bullied, how would you want others to respond? What can you do to offer that same kind of loving response to others?

# PRACTICING PERSEVERANCE

*Consider it pure joy, my brothers and sisters, whenever you face trials of many kinds, because you know that the testing of your faith produces perseverance. Let perseverance finish its work so that you may be mature and complete, not lacking anything.*

JAMES 1:2–4

When runners train for marathons, they don't start by running the full distance right away. They start with two miles one week and then three the next, working up to their eventual goal. This is similar to how we, as Christians, practice perseverance.

James reminded believers that everyone faces challenges. Sometimes, your parents might experience financial troubles. Or you might struggle with bouts of anxiety. These tough times are a natural part of life, and James urged the members of the early church to be joyful when they were living through them. Our faith is tested during the hard times, but challenges build our endurance, ensuring that we do not give up in our pursuit of God.

Hard days can make you feel like no one understands you. But you can receive the benefit of perseverance—just like a runner training for a long race—when you rely on God and His strength to support you. God understands you and stands by your side. Weathering tough challenges with His support can help you grow, learn, and be ready for tomorrow.

Persevering in our faith isn't always easy. However, being strong in times of trouble builds us into the people God desires us to be.

REFLECT

What challenges have you or your family had to work through? Did you find ways to turn to God when things were hard?

_____

_____

_____

# LIVING SACRIFICIALLY

*Therefore, I urge you, brothers and sisters, in view of God's mercy, to offer your bodies as a living sacrifice, holy and pleasing to God— this is your true and proper worship.*

**ROMANS 12:1**

Sacrifices—giving up something we want in order to contribute to something greater—are hard. But we make them daily. You might give up time with friends to practice piano. Or maybe you cut down on social media so that you have time to study each night.

Just like you make sacrifices in your life, Christians throughout history made sacrifices, too. When someone sinned in the Old Testament, believers sacrificed an animal to ask for forgiveness. Eventually, Jesus became the ultimate living sacrifice. His death on the Cross paid for the sins of humanity forever, ending the need for animal sacrifice.

Now, we are each called to be a different kind of living sacrifice by offering our spirits to God. This means acting in a way that is pleasing to God, instead of acting in ways that are just easy or feel good.

Living a life of sacrifice can include obeying your parents even when you don't want to. It might mean resisting the urge to spread rumors. It might mean going out of your way to show kindness to someone who has hurt you.

We demonstrate sacrifice by setting aside our own desires in order to do what is good. It might not be fun or convenient. However, it is worth it to help share God's love and to show our gratitude for His gifts in our lives.

**REFLECT**

What things have you sacrificed in the past? What are some things that would be very hard for you to share or give up for God?

_____

_____

_____

# LETTING GO OF ENVY

So then, just as you received Christ Jesus as Lord, continue to live your lives in Him, rooted and built up in Him, strengthened in the faith as you were taught, and overflowing with thankfulness.

COLOSSIANS 2:6–7

Envy is an all-consuming emotion. You might feel it when you compare someone's brand new phone to your outdated one or when a friend is on a lavish vacation while you're stuck at home. Envy is a painful realization that others have something that we desperately want. It can even stir up a lot of other emotions, like anger, sadness, or fear. In the book of Proverbs, King Solomon describes envy as a powerful emotion that can rot the very core of who we are.

When we compare our possessions or circumstances to those of others, we often experience resentment. It is difficult to feel grateful for what we have while we are eyeing someone else's stuff. This desire for others' blessings blinds us to the gifts God has given us. Envy chokes our contentment and destroys our peace.

The only way to combat envy is to live a life of gratitude. When you start to feel jealous of others' possessions, stop to thank the Lord for every gift He's given you. This will bring peace to your heart. When you actively choose to count your blessings rather than be envious, you can enjoy life to its fullest.

REFLECT

What or who makes you feel envious? To prepare for the next time you feel envy, brainstorm a few ways that you can remind yourself of all the things you are grateful for.

# LIVING IN THE SPIRIT

*But the fruit of the Spirit is love, joy, peace, forbearance, kindness, goodness, faithfulness, gentleness, and self-control. Against such things there is no law.*

**GALATIANS 5:22–23**

When we ask Jesus for forgiveness, we immediately receive the Holy Spirit. The Holy Spirit—the spirit of God, which lives within believers—forgives our sin and comforts us when we are in pain.

The Bible uses fruit as a way to help us understand what the Holy Spirit brings into our lives. The Holy Spirit plants fruit in our souls: the fruit of love, joy, peace, patience, kindness, goodness, faithfulness, gentleness, and self-control. These qualities—the fruit of the Spirit—take root in our souls when we choose to walk in the Spirit instead of our sin. They result from God's presence in our lives, changing us from the inside out.

Eventually, this fruit overflows into our everyday actions. We have love in our lives because God loves us. We understand what kindness is because of His kindness toward us. God easily gives us these qualities because He embodies all of them.

The next time you begin to feel impatient, ask the Lord to give you patience. When you are struggling with sin, pray for the Holy Spirit to give you self-control. Asking for God's help and inviting Him in makes room for the Lord to cultivate these fruits.

REFLECT

Which of these fruits are evident in your life? Which fruits do you need to ask the Holy Spirit to grow within you?

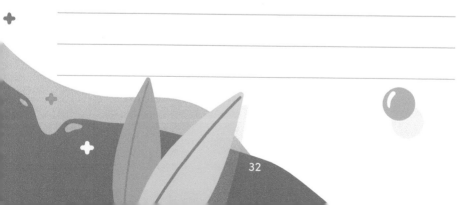

# WORSHIPPING THE LORD

*Worship the Lord in the splendor of His holiness.*

PSALM 29:2

Worship is a spiritual practice that gives God the glory He deserves. The music portion of a church service is a great example of worship. Whether your church plays contemporary songs or older hymns, that time is dedicated to celebrating the Lord with other believers. The heart of worship is praising God for who He is. We have so many reasons to thank Him.

In Psalm 29, King David wrote several reasons we should offer praises to God. He is the God of all glory and strength. The Lord's holiness is magnificent. God's voice is powerful. He sits enthroned as King and blesses His people with peace. These are only a few of the qualities of God's goodness, and we could spend a lifetime praising Him for these alone.

The next time you hear a worship song, try really listening to the words instead of just singing along. Treasure the truth that you hear about God. Then, thank Him for being the kind, holy, and mighty God described by David in Psalm 29.

Though you can worship God by singing in a sanctuary, worship doesn't always require our voices. We worship God when we work hard for our grades. We worship when we turn to God in prayer. Worship can take many forms, but it always involves our hearts.

The way we worship God reflects our thankfulness for His love. Choose to honor Him in every aspect of your life today.

REFLECT

Since worship is a lifestyle, how can you incorporate praise into your every-day routine instead of just saving it for church?

_____

_____

_____

# HAVING A CRUSH

Feeling butterflies in your stomach is exciting, and everyone craves the experience of expressing affection and having it returned. Crushes are part of growing up, but the feelings can come and go quickly. It is possible to feel completely hooked on someone one week and be over them the next. It can also be easy to take a crush too far, into an unhealthy obsession.

Jesus knows that our hearts are the source of all our actions, so He asks us to be careful when we have crushes. Just as your heart pumps healthy blood through your veins, your spiritual heart infuses healthy emotions into your life. Flooding your heart with extreme but temporary feelings leaves room for disaster when the feelings fade away or disappoint you.

When it comes to protecting our hearts, we need to learn from Samson's mistakes. Samson, a judge in Israelite history, fell hard for a girl. He acted on his emotions, which were more about attraction than devotion. Because he didn't guard his heart, Samson ended up harming his heart and his walk with God—all for a crush.

Christ advises us to protect ourselves from overly intense feelings. He invites us to exchange the fleeting feelings of a crush with the forever power of His love. Even when you are feeling the excitement of a crush, take some time each day to be quiet and anchor yourself in God's unchanging love for you.

REFLECT

What boundaries can you set to keep your heart safe when it comes to crushes?

# ENJOYING GOD'S CREATION

*When I consider Your heavens, the work of Your fingers, the moon and the stars, which You have set in place, what is mankind that You are mindful of them, human beings that You care for them?*

PSALM 8:3–4

It's truly incredible to think about everything God created. Every corner of Earth has unique animals, from the polar bears and orca whales of the Arctic to the lions and hippos of sub-Saharan Africa. And not only did God fill creation with diversity; He also designed it with great detail.

We see the creative hand of God in nature, but nature also reminds us of how small we are in comparison to the Lord. We could never create something as magnificent as the Grand Canyon or as beautiful as blooming flowers. We don't have the power to produce the depths of the oceans or hang the moon and stars. When we consider all God has created in this world, it's astonishing to know He chooses to have a relationship with us.

Seeing God's creations can help us worship Him. Be intentional about spending some time outside. Go for a prayer walk throughout your neighborhood and thank the Lord for creating every flower, tree, and squirrel you see. Ultimately, the Lord gave intricate details to every aspect of nature because He lovingly created it. Let's praise Him for the gift of His beautiful creation.

REFLECT

What aspects of God's creation do you enjoy? What activities in your life help you rejoice in the wonder of God's creation?

# WORKING HARD

*All hard work brings a profit, but mere talk leads only to poverty.*

PROVERBS 14:23

Have you ever quit something because it felt too hard? A sport that sounded fun but was actually tough to master? A hobby that took more effort than you expected? Most of us have experienced this. But when we give something all we've got, our determination pays off.

In Proverbs, King Solomon noted that we always profit from hard work. Hard work doesn't guarantee that we will be the richest or most successful. Instead, it helps us develop a great work ethic. When we complete a task, we can take pride and joy in knowing we did our job. Hard work teaches us responsibility and grows our determination. From scrubbing a toilet to crafting a prize-winning science project, our hard work reflects our character, whether or not anyone is watching.

If we refuse to work hard, we lose the joy of stretching our character and abilities. For instance, maybe you started to play the guitar because you thought it sounded beautiful. After practicing a few times, you found yourself struggling to form chords. You might feel discouraged and tempted to quit instead of pushing through defeat. But if you quit, you'll lose the opportunity to enjoy playing music for yourself and others.

The next time you find yourself struggling to complete a task, remember that hard work is just that: hard! But it's always of great benefit to us, and we, as Christ's followers, can use our work ethic as another way to worship the Lord.

REFLECT

What benefits have you gained through working hard?

# EXPERIENCING LOSS

*The Lord is close to the brokenhearted
and saves those who are crushed in spirit.*

PSALM 34:18

Grief is the overpowering sense of sadness that we feel when something or someone that we care about deeply is lost. Unfortunately, everyone experiences grief, though we all handle it differently, and grieve different things. But, no matter why you are grieving, God promises to be near.

In the Bible, this truth became clear to David when King Saul tried to kill him. David went on the run, asking surrounding nations for protection, with no luck. Afraid for his life, David wrote about the Lord's faithfulness despite his own incredible sadness. In Psalm 34, he reminded himself that God is close to the brokenhearted. The Lord saves those whose spirits are crushed.

When we are filled with sadness, running to the Lord isn't always our natural reaction. Sometimes we forget that love and comfort are waiting for us. Luckily, when we do decide to turn to God in our grief, we don't have to go very far.

God was there to support David when he fled for his life, and God is also there for you when you need comfort. The Lord already knows the sadness in your heart. Let His presence and His power support you when you feel broken. God doesn't promise to make our lives perfect, but He promises to be there for the healing process. Turn to God with your prayers and pain. Allow the Lord to hold you up when life crushes you.

REFLECT
When have you experienced a broken heart? How did God's presence comfort you?

# ACCEPTING GOD'S GRACE

*For it is by grace you have been saved, through
faith—and this is not from yourselves, it is the gift
of God—not by works, so that no one can boast.*

EPHESIANS 2:8–9

Think of the last time you worked hard for something. Maybe you practiced a solo over and over again to make the school musical. Or perhaps you swam hundreds of laps in the pool so that you could perform well at an upcoming swim meet. We work hard for the things we want. However, Scripture tells us that there's one thing we can't achieve through hard work: God's grace. He gives it to us as a gift.

Grace is the acceptance and love that we receive from Christ, no matter what. We don't have to work for or earn the favor of God. It is given to us through Christ's death on the Cross. The Lord forgives us and allows us to have a relationship with Him, even when we've messed up. Therefore, we shouldn't brag about the grace we've received. Since it is a gift we did not earn, we should receive it with gratitude and humility and then share it with others.

The best response to receiving God's grace is to accept it every day. When you struggle to forgive yourself for past mistakes, let grace remind you that you are forgiven. If you feel unloved, remember God's great love for you. Nothing excludes you from receiving His loving-kindness. Rejoice in being given grace and love!

### REFLECT

Do you ever feel like you need to earn God's grace?

# TAKING TIME TO REST

*Come to me, all you who are weary and burdened,
and I will give you rest.*

MATTHEW 11:28

Our schedules are so packed with school, friends, family, chores, jobs, and hobbies, it can be hard to find time to take a break. Luckily, instead of asking us to work constantly, the Lord invites us to periodically stop our routines and find the physical and spiritual rest that we need.

Throughout Scripture, God gives us different examples of what rest can look like. God created the heavens, the Earth, and people in six days, and He rested on the seventh day to enjoy His creation. Scripture refers to this day of rest as *Sabbath*. Centuries later, we see this idea pop up in the Ten Commandments. God's people were commanded to "remember the Sabbath day by keeping it holy" (Exodus 20:8). And when Jesus comforts those who are tired and worried in the New Testament, He promises to give us spiritual rest for our weary hearts.

These examples show the importance of finding balance in our lives. While hard work is good, taking a day off, or even finding a few minutes to slow down, is a chance to break from our rushed routines. It recharges our hearts so that we have the energy to accomplish our work, and it resets our minds to focus on the Lord.

Rest is an invitation to slow down and enjoy the blessings God has given us. It sometimes feels like there is no room for rest in our busy world, but rest is a gift from God, who knows us best.

REFLECT

How do you rest throughout the week? How do you feel after taking some quiet time to spend with God?

# SUPPORTING YOUR FRIENDS

*Though one may be overpowered, two can defend themselves.*
*A cord of three strands is not quickly broken.*

ECCLESIASTES 4:12

If you've had friends show up to your volleyball game or band concert to cheer you on, you know how meaningful support can be. When friends are truly supportive, they encourage you to use your gifts and strengths for God's glory. When you are stressed, they know what to say to help you feel better. Acts of support don't have to be big in order to matter. Whether we offer physical, emotional, or spiritual support, loving our friends well is a result of knowing Jesus deeply. We love our friends because Jesus loves us.

In the book of Ecclesiastes, King Solomon was questioning the meaning of life. As he searched for answers, he realized the importance of thriving friendships. He compared friendships to a cord, or rope, braided together. If a rope is woven together with other ropes, it becomes stronger. It can bear more weight and tension. Likewise, when we rely on friends, they can support us when we are stressed or tired.

We don't have to live life alone. We can encourage our friends and rely on them to do the same for us. The next time you see a friend struggling, choose to strengthen them in their time of need. Friendships are give-and-take, meaning sometimes you'll be giving support and sometimes you'll be receiving it. Either way, God guides us to help our friends.

REFLECT

How has support from a friend encouraged you? How can you support a friend today?

_____

_____

_____

# SEEING INNER BEAUTY

*Your beauty should not come from outward adornment, such as elaborate hairstyles and the wearing of gold jewelry or fine clothes. Rather, it should be that of your inner self, the unfading beauty of a gentle and quiet spirit, which is of great worth in God's sight.*

1 PETER 3:3–4

When we think of beauty, we usually think of physical appearance— things like a slim figure, clear skin, or pearly white teeth. It's tempting to believe our beauty is only skin-deep, but Christ defines beauty very differently from how the world does. The world is full of ever-changing fashion trends and makeup styles, but beauty as God defines it never fades or goes out of style.

Thousands of years ago, when Peter wrote to local believers, he challenged Christian women to flip their idea of beauty inside out. He redefined being beautiful as having a gentle, quiet spirit and practicing God's example of humility. This version of beauty boasts of the power of the Cross and puts all confidence in Christ, rather than in worldly trends. Inner beauty is the natural overflow of God's goodness. People who radiate inner beauty make the people around them feel loved, seen, and cherished, just as Christ loves and cherishes us. No one can steal this kind of beauty from us or tell us it's outdated.

The next time you stand in front of the mirror, you can still fix any unruly hairs or makeup blunders, but know that your beauty is more than the reflection in the mirror. Choose to reflect inner beauty by sharing God's love with those around you.

REFLECT

What are some ways you can radiate the love of Christ and, thus, inner beauty, today?

# LIVING HOPEFULLY

Praise be to the God and Father of our Lord Jesus Christ!
In His great mercy He has given us new birth into a living hope
through the resurrection of Jesus Christ from the dead, and
into an inheritance that can never perish, spoil, or fade.

**1 PETER 1:3–4**

Hope can be big or small. Sometimes, you hope for little things, like passing a test or having tacos for dinner. Other times, you hope for something bigger—for an argument with a friend to resolve quickly or for a sick family member to get better. As believers, our hope is anchored in the confidence that God loves us and will work for our good. Scripture reminds us that we receive strength by putting our hope in God (Isaiah 40:31). We might suffer in this life, but God's hope will never disappoint us (Romans 5:5). The feelings of confidence and joy that are inspired by hope overflow into our lives through the power of the Holy Spirit (Romans 15:13). Our Lord is the God of hope.

God created hope through the Gospel and has given it to us, His children. No one can steal it. It can never fade. God's promise of Heaven is protected. Still, when we are afraid or sad, it can be tough to remember the promises that God has made to us.

When you feel lost or unhopeful, turn to the Gospel. It will remind you that God's grace is a gift, not something you have to earn. Even when you're dealing with difficult circumstances or defeat in your daily life, you have the constant hope that Christ loves you, redeems you, and gives you eternal life. Nothing can ever change that.

REFLECT

Have you encountered tough challenges that made you lose sight of God's hope?

# NAVIGATING CHANGE

We all experience changes. Our classes get more difficult, our bodies develop, and some of our friendships come and go. You might feel afraid of or frustrated by new changes, but the Lord's constant presence can bring you peace.

Throughout the Bible, God never changes. He was trustworthy thousands of years ago, and He will continue to be forever. When we experience unwanted change, God's consistency gives us hope. He will continue to be faithful through uncertain circumstances. Not only is God consistent, but He's always in control. God is not surprised by changes to our situation or confused by what's going on.

It can be hard to adjust to change. But change also brings us things we never dreamed of. For instance, moving to a new city might feel scary, but it might also bring the joy of meeting your new best friend. Moving up to a new grade in school can be a big change, but it can also introduce you to new subjects that you enjoy. Jesus is always working for our good, even in unexpected circumstances.

The next time a big change comes around, acknowledge how you feel about it. Embrace the changes in your life, but also know that it's okay to grieve when something old leaves your life to make way for something new. Remember that Christ is forever the same. His support and love will be there through every change you face.

REFLECT

When have you experienced a change in your life? How did God's unchanging character comfort you during this time?

_____

_____

_____

# FEELING LEFT OUT

For I am convinced that neither death nor life, neither angels nor demons, neither the present nor the future, nor any powers, neither height nor depth, nor anything else in all creation, will be able to separate us from the love of God that is in Christ Jesus our Lord.

ROMANS 8:38–39

Being left out feels terrible. Though you might feel alone with this pain, God's love for us never changes. There is nothing that can separate us from it. It anchors us when our circumstances and emotions try to tell us that we aren't loved.

Being left out can stir up all of your fears and insecurities, making you feel vulnerable and unwanted. You can't change these circumstances, but you can choose your reaction to them. Feeling discouraged or disappointed is a natural response to being excluded, but if you aren't careful, this frustration can lead to bitterness and anger. In these moments, we must remind ourselves that a lost invitation or an exclusive clique can't threaten our status as a loved child of God.

Though you might feel like you're the only person being left out, odds are that there is someone around you who feels excluded, too. Instead of becoming distracted with disappointment, love those who are also left out. Invite a person who sits by themselves to join you at lunch. Look for those who don't have many friends. Knowing nothing can separate us from God's love should encourage us to invite others into His love as well. Though it feels lonely to be left out, God's love reminds us we are not alone.

REFLECT

What emotions do you feel when you are left out? What can you do to make someone else feel included today?

_____

_____

_____

# PLAYING YOUR ROLE IN THE CHURCH

*Now you are the body of Christ, and each one of you is a part of it.*

**1 CORINTHIANS 12:27**

Think about all the different parts that make up the human body. Each part serves a unique purpose, and while some parts play a bigger role in our bodies than others, they all work together to help us live. Your lungs help you breathe, while your elbows allow you to bend your arms. Every part is needed.

Just as each organ plays its own role in our physical bodies, each believer has a role in the spiritual body of Christ, the Church. Some have the gift of teaching, which helps others know more about the Bible and God. Others have the gift of evangelism, which means they easily share with others the good news of the Gospel. Other spiritual gifts include serving, giving generously, and showing mercy. These roles work together to build the local church.

Just like our bodies can be thrown out of whack when one part isn't working correctly, the church suffers if some of us fail to actively contribute. Every follower of Christ has a part to play in the church, regardless of what spiritual gifts they have. There might be someone in your small group who is deeply discouraged. Your gift of encouragement can lift their spirits at a time when they need it most. Maybe you could host a weekly Bible study where your gift of hospitality makes a friend feel loved and supported.

You are not a spare part. The Holy Spirit has gifted you with the right tools to fill the needs of the Church.

**REFLECT**

What spiritual gifts do you have? How can you use them to benefit the Church?

_____

_____

_____

# PURSUING HOLINESS

*But just as He who called you is holy, so be holy in all you do;*
*for it is written: "Be holy, because I am holy."*

1 PETER 1:15–16

Have you ever done something just because it was trendy? Maybe you wear your hair in a specific style because girls from school wear it like that. It's easy to imitate others in life, but spiritually, God wants us to be more like Him. We have a call as believers to be different.

Holiness is a spiritual term that means our actions, words, and lives should look more like Jesus's life than the examples in the world around us. In the Old Testament, God commanded His people, the Israelites, to be holy. He wanted them to be different from other nations, who lived selfishly. He wanted His people to behave differently because He is different.

Today, we are still called to live like the Lord instead of trying to blend in with the world. Being holy as God is holy will make us different. We'll show kindness when the world shows hate. We'll be generous when others are stingy.

Ultimately, God's character defines holiness. He is perfect, pure, and powerful. Though we will not be perfect like God, the better we know him, the more we will reflect Jesus's character.

It isn't always easy to act in a way that is holy. Sometimes, it feels a lot simpler to stay quiet when we see something wrong or to put our needs above the needs of others. However, God's love gives us the strength to do what is right, to set an example for the people around us, and to display His character to those around us.

REFLECT

Write down some words to describe God's holiness. How can you follow God's example?

_____

_____

_____

# CHOOSING YOUR FRIENDS

*Walk with the wise and become wise,*
*for a companion of fools suffers harm.*

PROVERBS 13:20

How have your friends impacted your life? They've probably given you great joy and lots of laughs. But friendship is more than just fun. Friends also influence the decisions we make, so we need to choose our friendships wisely.

In the book of Proverbs, King Solomon teaches us that when we surround ourselves with friends who follow God's Word, we benefit from the good choices they make. In group settings, these are the people who stand up for the right thing, even if it costs them.

King Solomon also taught that choosing friends who aren't wise can bring us harm. If a friend has ever convinced you to do something that got you grounded, you know how true King Solomon's teaching is. When friends lack wisdom, they choose doing what they want—like disobeying a parent or disrespecting a teacher—over doing what's right. If you follow in their footsteps, you pay for the consequences of their careless actions.

Ultimately, you can either surround yourself with people who follow Christ's example, or you can hang out with people who stir up trouble. Either way, there are consequences for your actions. That's why it's important to think about your friendships and how they make you act. If certain friends discourage you from doing what you know is right, it's time to distance yourself from their harmful habits. Instead, choose wise friends who challenge you to live a godly life.

REFLECT

How has a friend's wisdom encouraged you to live wisely?

_____

_____

_____

# CALMING ANXIOUS THOUGHTS

When I said, "My foot is slipping," your unfailing love,
Lord, supported me. When anxiety was great within me,
your consolation brought me joy.

**PSALM 94:18–19**

When anxious thoughts swirl within us, they build off of our worries, replacing rational concerns with the feeling of being totally overwhelmed. The author of Psalm 94 described this experience like the ground beneath him crumbling, his foot slipping. Everyone experiences this kind of unease. Although it can flood our heads, anxiety doesn't have to drown us. When the world around us seems as if it's caving in, we can turn to the Lord's unfailing love. It will not shake or fail.

Reminding ourselves of the truth of God's support can help us separate fact from fiction when we feel anxious. Though we can't completely control the future, God's authority is trustworthy. His love supports us when doubt scares us.

If you've ever been encouraged by someone in times of pain or hurt, you know how helpful a hug, kind word, and prayer can be. God's comfort is even larger and more encompassing.

God knows the concerns of our hearts and helps us walk through them to find peace. Still, there are some circumstances where you might need more than spiritual support in order to overcome your anxiety. Talk to a trusted adult if you can't seem to shake the feeling of being overwhelmed, worried, or jittery.

REFLECT

What anxious thoughts pop up in your mind? What act of worship—a prayer, a walk, or a talk with someone you love—can help remind you of God's support?

# MEDITATING ON GOD'S GOODNESS

*. . . and I will meditate on Your wonderful works.*

PSALM 145:5

You might have heard of meditation before. While other religions incorporate it as a way to clear one's mind, biblical meditation reminds us about the character, commands, and comfort of God. It refreshes our hearts and reminds us of the reasons we can confidently trust Him.

One way to meditate on God's goodness is to look at the way He has been faithful to generations before us. In the Old Testament, after the Israelites became enslaved to Egypt, the Lord sent plagues to save them and split the Red Sea for them when they ran away. In the New Testament, God sent the greatest miracle of all, His Son, Jesus, to Earth. Throughout His ministry, Jesus healed people both spiritually and physically. He restored sight, brought people back to life, and died on the Cross to give eternal life to those who believe.

But we don't only have to look to the past. God continues to be mighty today. We see His hands at work when sick people start feeling better or when a crisis is averted. We feel God's presence when we experience love and joy.

There are many ways to meditate on God's goodness. You can write characteristics of the Lord on a notecard and hang it on your mirror. Sing songs of praise. Memorize Bible verses about God's love that speak to you. Make time in your day to focus on God's Word and celebrate His role in your life.

REFLECT

What miraculous things has the Lord done in your life?

_____

_____

_____

# BEING BRAVE

When we think of bravery, we might picture a soldier on the battlefield or a firefighter helping people escape a burning building. Risking your life for the sake of others is a high form of bravery, but we can be brave in our everyday lives, too. When we choose to do the hard thing or the thing that makes us most afraid, we display courage.

In the Old Testament, King David constantly found himself needing to be very brave. To find his courage, he didn't look at his own accomplishments but focused on the greatness of God. In Psalm 27, David reminded himself of who the Lord is: our light and salvation, a place of safety. If a situation is dark, Christ is our light. If a circumstance feels hopeless, God is our salvation. When you need a jolt of bravery, remind yourself of who God is, just like David did.

Being brave doesn't mean that our fear goes away. It means we place our confidence in God rather than in our own abilities. Though our friendships, schoolwork, and family situations can make us feel afraid, nothing can shake the Lord.

Choosing to be brave is just that: a choice. This world needs you to show fierce courage and stand up for truth and love. We need your strength, even when it's scary. Being brave might be hard, but it makes us holy. So do the hard thing today. Be bold. Be brave.

REFLECT
What scares you? When you imagine yourself being brave, what do you see?

# PLACING CONFIDENCE IN GOD

*But blessed is the one who trusts in the Lord,*
*whose confidence is in Him.*

JEREMIAH 17:7

When you think of confidence, you probably think of the self-confidence you get from your beauty, talent, and circumstances. Feeling confident about the talents and gifts that God gave us is a wonderful way to celebrate His love. Still, though, these gifts from God might fade or change. But His love always stays the same. Jeremiah 17:7 promises a blessing when we trust in the Lord.

Scripture gives us several reasons why we can fully trust God. Through faith in Jesus, "we may approach God with freedom and confidence" (Ephesians 3:12). We can draw near to "God's throne of grace with confidence, so that we may receive mercy and find grace to help us in our time of need" (Hebrews 4:16). 1 John 5:14 says, "This is the confidence we have in approaching God: that if we ask anything according to His will, He hears us." We can be confident that God began a good work in us and will complete it (Philippians 1:6). These truths are unshakable and unmovable. We can always depend on God for these things.

It might be tempting to use our looks or grades as a source of confidence, but a bad hair day or low grade can easily crush our spirits. Ultimately, the Lord's unchanging character is the only thing we can trust to never change or fail us. Let's anchor our hope in God today. Through trusting Him, we will receive the blessing of His presence and His grace.

REFLECT
Why can you place confidence in Christ?

# UNDERSTANDING FAITH

*Now faith is confidence in what we hope for
and assurance about what we do not see.*

**HEBREWS 11:1**

We can put our hope in many different things. We can have faith that we studied enough to pass a history quiz or believe we have enough strength to get ourselves through hard times. But if we are not careful, we can let our talents, grades, and popularity define us and give us hope. As believers, we must instead place our confidence in Christ. The most important aspect of our Christian life is our faith in Jesus.

Hebrews 11:1 gives us a simple definition of faith: trust and hope that what God says is true. This confidence assures us that God is present. Though we cannot see God, we know He's real from the way He's been present in our lives. We know our sin separated us from God, but through Christ's death on the Cross, we receive forgiveness of our sins. Our trust in God confirms Heaven is a place where we will one day reunite with Him. Faith is essential to our salvation. It anchors us as we go through hard changes because God remains the same.

Someone who has faith in Jesus faithfully follows Him. You can have faith that God will be with you during a loved one's battle with illness. You can know God loves and cares for you, even when you mess up. By trusting God's promises, we stay connected to Him through faith. Choose to live a life of faith by knowing God is trustworthy.

REFLECT

Why do you trust Jesus? How does this faith comfort you?

_____

_____

_____

# SHARING THE GOSPEL

Everyone loves to hear good news—that your team won the game or that your friend can sleep over at your house Friday night. But God's message of love and forgiveness is the best news any of us will ever hear. The Gospel is an incredible gift because it changes every aspect of our lives.

The apostle Paul knew this to be true. After spending most of his life persecuting Christians, Paul eventually learned about Jesus. God's forgiveness changed him forever. He knew that if God could forgive someone like him, the Lord could forgive anyone. Paul lived the rest of his years teaching the Gospel to everyone he met.

When Paul wrote to believers in Rome, he reminded them of the vital role they played in sharing the message of the Gospel, a role that Christians still play today. People cannot believe in something they've never heard of. Jesus invites us to not only to receive His love but also to share it with those around us.

Sometimes, we let fear stop us from sharing the Gospel with friends. You might be afraid of what they'll think of your relationship with Jesus or not feel prepared to answer their questions about your faith. It's okay to be afraid, but you shouldn't let that stop you. Start by sharing a favorite Bible verse with a friend, and see where it goes from there. Let your faith in Jesus help you tell others about the hope found in Christ.

REFLECT
Why do you want to share Christ's love and hope with others?

# USING YOUR TIME WISELY

*Be very careful, then, how you live—not as unwise but as wise,
making the most of every opportunity, because the days are evil.*

EPHESIANS 5:15–16

If we're honest, most of our free time probably involves some type of screen. We plop in front of the TV to catch up on new episodes of our favorite shows while scrolling through social media on our phones. Although there is nothing wrong with enjoying a movie or spending time on our devices, it's not always the wisest use of our time. And God wants us to make the most of every opportunity we have.

In the early church, Paul instructed believers not to waste a single second of their time. He encouraged them to use every moment for God's glory and to use wisdom to make the most of every opportunity. Instead of choosing the most comfortable thing, wisdom challenges us to do what we know is right. A wise mind-set pushes us to come home from school and spend time with the Lord or obediently finish our chores, instead of watching TV. We glorify the Lord when we choose to use our time for Him, not just for ourselves.

Though our schedules can quickly fill up with school, church, and extracurricular activities, there are always ways we can serve. Maybe you can babysit the younger kids who live next door while their parents go to the grocery store. Or you might use your time wisely by leading a Bible study before or after school each week. God has given us this life; let's make the most of it.

REFLECT

How do you typically spend your free time?

_____

_____

_____

# BEING PATIENT

Be completely humble and gentle; be patient,
bearing with one another in love.

EPHESIANS 4:2

Sometimes, we grow impatient while waiting in line or dealing with a frustrating sibling. Regardless of what tempts us to lose our temper, we must learn to practice patience.

In the New Testament, Paul encouraged believers to connect to others by acting with humility, gentleness, and patience. He knew the church community would suffer if pride, anger, and impatience were present. The same is true for us today. Our relationships won't grow if we continually lose our patience.

Selfishness is the root cause of impatience. You might feel impatient in a long line in the cafeteria. But it is not the long line that is really upsetting you; it is that you will have less time to hang out with your friends during lunch. You're feeling impatient because you might not get what you want. This kind of selfish impatience happens to everyone, but it can get in the way of living like Jesus. It is hard to love those around you when you are grumbling about your circumstances instead of showing gratitude for your blessings.

Ultimately, patience grows in us through the Holy Spirit's help. It develops as we spend time with the Lord, who graciously shows patience to us. As we learn to control our tempers, we realize the world doesn't revolve around us. So, the next time you want to blow up at a younger sibling, practice patience instead of responding in anger, and show the power of God working in your life.

REFLECT

How can being more patient with your family and friends help your relationships grow stronger?

_____

_____

_____

# FACING DISAPPOINTMENT

*I have told you these things, so that in me you may have peace.*
*In this world you will have trouble. But take heart!*
*I have overcome the world.*

Disappointment is the feeling of defeat you get when things don't end up the way you'd hoped. You might feel disappointed when you work hard for something and still don't accomplish it. You also might feel disappointed if a friend's actions let you down. The Bible tells us that Jesus knows that we will experience hardships. Everyone experiences the pain of unmet expectations.

However, we can choose to respond to our disappointment in a healthy way by being honest with the Lord. He promises to hear all of our prayers and requests. Let Him know when you are hurting and feeling frustrated. God will help carry your burden and remind you that He has a plan for you, in spite of these setbacks. When we shift our focus off of our plan and onto the Lord's plan, we experience peace. This action reminds us God can overcome any obstacle in our lives.

You might not understand why you are going through a discouraging circumstance. When a dream or expectation fails you, remember that the Lord never will. Use times of disappointment as an opportunity to rely on the Lord instead of your own understanding. You will always have trouble in this world, but the Lord promises us peace.

REFLECT

What makes you feel disappointed? When you are feeling down, do you share your disappointment with God? How about with a trusted adult or friend?

# RESPECTING OUR GUARDIANS

*Children, obey your parents in the Lord, for this is right.*

EPHESIANS 6:1

Some of us are raised by parents and stepparents, while others live with grandparents or other guardians. Even though our family dynamics might be unique, the Bible is clear that we all must love and respect our caretakers by obeying them.

When the disciple Paul wrote to Christians in the early church, he described how a Christian household should act: husbands were instructed to love their wives, wives to respect their husbands, and children to obey their parents. We are commanded to respect and obey our guardians.

Sometimes, it's tempting to believe we know better than the people in charge. But adults have more experience, and they wisely know what's best for us. When we fail to obey our guardians, they may discipline us. This discipline doesn't come from meanness but from a desire to teach an important lesson.

Every time you respect authority figures in your life, you honor the Lord. Keep that in mind the next time you don't want to vacuum the carpet or clean your bathroom!

However, if a guardian or adult ever asks you to do something that's harmful to you or to others, you don't have to suffer abuse, and you should not abuse others. Immediately find a trusted teacher, pastor, or parent of a friend to help.

REFLECT

Have your parents or guardians ever helped you through a situation that you didn't know how to handle?

---

---

---

# ASKING FOR HELP

God is our refuge and strength, an ever-present help in trouble.

PSALM 46:1

Do you have a hard time asking for help? Sometimes it can feel like a sign of weakness. Yet none of us can make it through the world alone, especially without the Lord. The sooner we understand that asking for help is actually a strength, the quicker we can witness God's victory in our lives.

Psalm 46 describes the Lord's character—things that are true no matter what challenges you might face. This verse reminds us that God is our shelter, our protection, and always close. In the chaos of life, the Lord is a strong fortress. The writer also notes that the Lord is our strength. When we face challenges that make us feel small and weak, God's bravery strengthens us.

Trouble always surrounds us. Sometimes, the ups and downs of life make it feel like we are stuck. The psalmist wrote that when he felt overwhelmed, it felt like the world was falling down around him: "Therefore we will not fear, though the earth give way and the mountains fall into the heart of the sea, though its waters roar and foam and the mountains quake with their surging" (Psalm 46:2–3). When the world around us seems like it's caving in, the Lord is an ever-present help.

Do you have a loved one who is sick? God is your refuge. Are you tired of family fights? The Lord is your strength. No matter what challenges we face, the Lord is *ours*. Ask for help in your problems. He is always there for you.

REFLECT

What challenges have you faced recently? How can you ask God for help in these situations?

_____

_____

_____

# FACING TEMPTATION

*No temptation has overtaken you except what is common to mankind. And God is faithful; He will not let you be tempted beyond what you can bear. But when you are tempted, He will also provide a way out so that you can endure it.*

**1 CORINTHIANS 10:13**

Every person on the planet has faced some sort of temptation. You may have been tempted to speak unkindly to someone who was bothering you or to disobey your parents when they asked you to do something uninteresting. But temptation distracts us from living like Jesus. Though getting past temptations can be overwhelming, God's Word promises us a way out. Jesus Himself modeled this for us.

When Jesus first started His ministry on Earth, He fasted for 40 days and nights in the desert. After a while, He was hungry, tired, and lonely. Satan tempted Jesus with food, praise, and glory, and told Jesus lies to confuse Him. But Jesus avoided the temptation by remembering the truth of Scripture. He knew what God wanted him to do because He knew and trusted God's Word. We should follow Jesus's example when we experience temptation to sin.

If you are often tempted to speak unkindly, memorize a Bible verse about the power of your speech. If it's hard for you to obey your parents' wishes, find some scriptures to encourage you next time you don't want to do your chores. As Paul reminded the church in Corinth, we are all sometimes tempted to choose what is easy instead of what is right, but God always provides us with a way out of sin.

REFLECT
What are your biggest temptations? Write down a Bible verse that can support you when you feel the desire to give in to temptation.

_____

_____

_____

Give thanks to the Lord, for He is good;
His love endures forever.

**PSALM 107:1**

After you receive a gift, it's considered a common courtesy to send a thank-you note. It expresses your thankfulness for a thoughtful present. When it comes to the blessings we receive from the Lord, though, we could never write an adequate thank-you. His gifts are too kind. But while our words fail to perfectly thank God, we can express our gratitude through the way we live our lives.

Everything you lay your eyes and your hands on is a gift from the Lord. The bed you slept on last night? It's from God. The orange juice you had at breakfast? Still God. From furniture to friends and family and everything in between, all you have is a gift from God, so thankfulness should always be on the tip of your tongue.

Greater than the material things we take for granted, however, are the direct blessings we receive spiritually through Christ. God made a way for us to be in His presence after sin separated us. Jesus died on the Cross and rose again because of our wrongdoing. Forgiveness and faith are both gifts we didn't earn, but we receive them anyway.

Today, let's live in constant awareness of the gifts around us. God's grace, goodness, and love endure forever. Take time regularly to praise the Lord, and your life will radiate contagious gratitude for God.

**REFLECT**

Write out the top five things you are grateful for right now. Spend some time in prayer, thanking Jesus for the blessings—both material and eternal—that we receive from Him.

*Mercy triumphs over judgment.*
JAMES 2:13

When someone shows us kindness we don't deserve, we receive their mercy. Mercy might look like a parent withholding punishment after you did something wrong or a teacher letting you retake a test that you failed. Out of all the blessings we have in Christ, His mercy is one of the greatest we receive. It is God showing compassion for us when we don't deserve His love.

An example of God's mercy is found in the parable of the unmerciful servant. In Matthew 18:21–35, Jesus tells the story of a servant who owed money to his master. After realizing his servant would never be able to pay what he owed, the master mercifully canceled his servant's debt. However, even after being forgiven, the servant did not extend the same mercy to a friend who owed him significantly less money. Once the master heard of his lack of forgiveness, he threw his servant into prison.

Our sin is like the servant's debt. There is nothing that we could do to repay God for the ways we've disobeyed Him. Christ died on the Cross to pay the penalty for our sin. Through His sacrifice, we receive mercy and forgiveness. Showing mercy to those around us is the best way we can express that we are grateful to Christ. When we realize all God has done for us, we can freely forgive those who wrong us. We can have more patience with younger siblings or people who irritate us. Choose the best response to God's gift of mercy by sharing it with others.

REFLECT
When did someone show you mercy? Can you think of a situation where you can show mercy to someone else?

_____

_____

_____

# FEELING OVERWHELMED

*Do not be anxious about anything, but in every situation, by prayer and petition, with thanksgiving, present your requests to God. And the peace of God, which transcends all understanding, will guard your hearts and your minds in Christ Jesus.*

When was the last time you felt overwhelmed? Maybe preparing for a big school project put extreme pressure on you. Or perhaps you don't know what to do about a difficult family situation. Sometimes our circumstances create chaos, but we can take comfort in knowing that Jesus can relate to being overwhelmed.

As the time grew closer for Jesus to die on the Cross, He told His disciples that He was troubled (Mark 14:33–34). Jesus was overwhelmed when He thought about the pain He would soon experience. Jesus turned to the Lord in prayer and invited His disciples to do the same. Jesus knew the Lord would comfort Him. This is still true for us today.

When we feel overwhelmed, our first response should be identical to Christ's. The Lord invites us to share the details of our rushed routines or hard homework with Him. He already knows why our hearts are overwhelmed, but He asks us to trust Him in the midst of it. When we trust Him, we receive peace that overcomes any situation we face.

Though life's circumstances can weigh heavily on us, we don't have to carry our burdens alone. Let's choose to turn to the Lord, who knows the troubles our hearts face and will comfort us in our chaos.

REFLECT
What makes you feel overwhelmed?

_____

_____

_____

# DOING YOUR BEST

And whatever you do, whether in word or deed, do it all in the name
of the Lord Jesus, giving thanks to God the Father through Him.

COLOSSIANS 3:17

Can you remember a time when you rushed to complete a project instead of working carefully? Maybe you were responsible for a household chore that was boring, and you rushed through it so that you could do something more fun. Sometimes we cut corners to complete a project instead of doing our best because it's easier and faster to do so. But if we are honest with ourselves, we usually get a sick feeling in the pit of our stomach when we don't do our best.

Giving 100 percent effort to the things we do and say gives glory to God. He doesn't require us to be perfect, but the Lord asks us to do our best because we are living examples of Him. In the New Testament, Paul wrote to the Colossian church about honoring God by doing everything for the Lord. There is no limit on what or how you can use your gifts for God's glory. Whatever you do—band, basketball, science club—the Lord asks that you do it all in His name, using your gifts to celebrate His love for you.

We don't have to be straight-A students or star athletes to do our best. Each of us has different skills. Instead of letting comparisons discourage you from doing your best, let gratitude drive your desire to glorify the Lord. Before you turn in a homework assignment, ask yourself if God would be pleased with your work. When you sweep the floor, do it as an act of worship. Doing our best gives God glory.

REFLECT

How do you feel when you do your best?

_____

_____

_____

# WANTING TO BE POPULAR

*Am I now trying to win the approval of human beings, or of God? Or am I trying to please people? If I were still trying to please people, I would not be a servant of Christ.*

GALATIANS 1:10

If we're honest, most of us have wanted to be popular at some point in our lives. We want others to love us and know who we are, and our desire to be loved is not wrong. But seeking attention can lead us to focus on ourselves rather than focusing on doing what is right.

When we find ourselves trying to earn the approval of the people around us instead of God's approval, our pride is motivating us. We are not alone in this temptation. Centuries ago, the apostle Paul had to warn believers in the Galatian church about pleasing people. If you've ever tried to live up to everyone's expectations, you know how tiresome and draining it can be. Not only is it exhausting to try, but it's impossible to please everyone.

When we long for popularity, we have gotten mixed up about our mission to love those around us and confused it with trying to be the most loved. When we prioritize and value God's love, our actions should help others find the same hope and joy in Christ. Instead of trying to be the funniest kid in your class, decide to be the most uplifting. Instead of wanting to be the most liked, choose to be the most loving. Instead of desiring to be seen, help others feel known. Serve God by serving others.

REFLECT

What makes someone popular? What do you think the difference is between being the most loving and being the most loved?

_____

_____

_____

# LIVING A LIFE OF DISCIPLESHIP

Therefore go and make disciples of all nations, baptizing them
in the name of the Father and of the Son and of the Holy Spirit,
and teaching them to obey everything I have commanded you.

MATTHEW 28:19-20

In science class, you can only learn so much by reading the text-book. To really understand the lessons, you need to watch the teacher perform an experiment. Seeing the lesson in action teaches you in a way that reading can't.

Jesus knew that people learn best by seeing examples. That's why He showed us how to live a godly life through discipleship— not just studying His teachings, but also living them.

During Jesus's ministry, He asked 12 men to follow Him as he healed the sick and gave sight to the blind. They gained wisdom by watching Jesus interact with others. After Jesus died on the Cross and rose three days later, He visited these 12 men and commanded them to do what He had done for them: teach others how to obey God through discipleship.

Discipleship might involve joining a Bible study group or con-necting with a church leader. You can learn how to better follow Christ by spending time with someone else who loves Him, too.

Discipleship also requires us to teach someone else. Encourage friends who are pursuing their own faith and make time to talk with them.

Discipleship is what Jesus taught us and expects of us. It is a joy to grow in your knowledge of Jesus with a community of other believers.

REFLECT
How has learning from others helped deepen your faith?

_____

_____

_____

# FEELING GUILTY

*Create in me a pure heart, O God,
and renew a steadfast spirit within me.*

**PSALM 51:10**

When was the last time you felt guilty? Maybe it was after you lied to a teacher or stole something from a sibling. When you mess up, your heart regrets the things you did or said. However, admitting you've done wrong isn't easy. Guilt can be overwhelming.

While it doesn't feel good, a guilty conscience is a healthy response to our wrongdoing. Guilt is a gift from God because it shows our need for His help. Christ washes our guilty consciences clean and gives us a fresh start.

It's important to remember that there is a difference between guilt and shame. Though we are all sinners, Jesus always forgives us. Guilt can lead us to repentance, but Satan turns our sin into shame. When this happens, the devil twists what we've done so that we start believing that the bad thing we did is who we are. Suddenly, we believe we're defined by our mistakes instead of God's grace. Guilt guides us to God, while shame stops us from seeking forgiveness.

The next time guilt weighs heavily on you, allow your regret to push you toward repentance. Apologize. Ask the Lord for forgiveness, and walk away from shame.

REFLECT

Have you ever felt guilty about something? Did apologizing for your actions help you move past your guilt?

# CHANGING FRIENDSHIPS

*One who has unreliable friends soon comes to ruin,*
*but there is a friend who sticks closer than a brother.*

Change is always difficult, but it can be especially tough when it comes to friendships. Our friendships shift naturally as our interests change. For instance, if you stop playing softball, you might not be as close to your teammates as you once were. But there are also more painful reasons that friendships change. It can feel devastating when you realize a friend has ditched you for a new crew. Seeing your friendships change is natural, but it can also be a really hard part of growing up.

King Solomon wrote about friendship quite frequently in the book of Proverbs. In chapter 18, he reflected on the difference between the number of friends we have and the quality of our friendships. He reminded us that it is more important to have a few close friends than it is to have lots of unreliable people in our lives.

Though it might hurt to let some friendships go, you can count on your deep friendships regardless of the circumstances. These kinds of friends stick by you through good and bad times, and they often feel more like family. In these friendships, both of you are anchored in God's love, choosing to navigate life together.

Remember that some friends will come and go and that there is a benefit in having fewer, deeper friendships. The next time you and a friend grow apart, be grateful for the sweet memories you created with one another.

REFLECT
Do you have a friendship that has changed as you have gotten older?

_____

_____

_____

# PRACTICING CHRIST'S HUMILITY

*Do nothing out of selfish ambition or vain conceit. Rather, in humility value others above yourselves, not looking to your own interests but each of you to the interests of the others.*

PHILIPPIANS 2:3–4

When you want something—even something small, like control of the remote or to sit in the front seat—it can be easy to get loud and emotional about your own desires, forgetting to honor the desires of the people around you. Thankfully, Christ has shown us how to practice humility.

As Paul sat in his jail cell, imprisoned for his faith in Jesus, he encouraged believers to embody Christ's spirit of humility and sacrifice. The Son of God showed us the ultimate example of humility when He came to Earth to die on the Cross so that humanity's sins could be forgiven. Christ left the comfort of Heaven to pave the way for us to go there. When we reflect on the weight of this sacrifice, we can become inspired by Christ's humility and mirror that humility to others.

Your personal desires and needs will always be present, but you must challenge yourself to put other people's needs, both great and small, before your own. If Jesus, the King of Kings, served others, we should also seek to serve instead of being served. Mirror Jesus's humility by giving up the front seat so that your sibling might be more comfortable or by letting someone else choose what's on TV.

REFLECT
How does Christ's humility encourage you to put others first?

# COMPARING YOURSELF TO OTHERS

*A heart at peace gives life to the body, but envy rots the bones.*

PROVERBS 14:30

We all compare ourselves to others. Sometimes, this can be a good thing. When you contrast your strengths to those of others, you learn where you have room to grow. But when you focus on what they have that you don't, it can fill you with envy and desire rather than optimism or hope. Maybe you know what it feels like to be jealous of someone, the way envy can make us forget our joy and "rots the bones," as Scripture puts it. When you are jealous, you end up spending your time trying to be like someone else instead of being who God made you to be.

Though others might be similar to you, no one is *exactly* like you. The Lord specifically gifted you with your talents. You serve a purpose in the body of Christ, a purpose that only you can fill. But when we get overly concerned with comparing ourselves to others, we forfeit the joy of being made one of a kind by God.

When you compare yourself to your friends or people you see on social media, you are attempting to understand your identity in the light of those people. Remember that your identity is always secure in Christ. When you feel envious or jealous of someone, take some time to meditate on the truths of God's love and His unique plan for you. God's Word sets us free from the jealousy we feel when we try to measure up to others. When we are at peace with how God has created us, we live a life of joy.

REFLECT

What areas of your life do you compare most to others? Have you ever felt envious or jealous of someone else's gifts? Write down a scripture to remind you of the gifts God has given you when you need reassurance.

_____

_____

_____

# MANAGING STRONG EMOTIONS

*Fools give full vent to their rage, but the wise bring calm in the end.*

**PROVERBS 29:11**

Emotions can be hard to handle. They wash over us suddenly and often with great intensity. However, just because you are feeling annoyed or disappointed doesn't mean you should let your feelings overtake you. With wisdom, you can manage strong emotions.

Proverbs 29 offers some direction on how to handle chaotic feelings. When you feel a strong emotion coming on, you have a choice: you can be in control of your emotions, or they can control you. When you don't manage your feelings, you might say things you don't really mean, and you might point your misplaced frustration at the people you love the most. Just because you are tired or sad doesn't mean you should take your feelings out on those around you. We need to express our feelings but in a healthy and productive way.

Imagine coming home after a bad day at school. You are exhausted and your siblings are bugging you. You have a choice to make. You can vent all of your frustration from the day at others, yelling hurtful words at them. Or you can ask for some privacy and spend some time alone until you've calmed down.

Next time you feel anger bubbling up inside you, take a minute to breathe. Leave the room, take a deep breath, say a prayer. When your strong feelings finally settle down, talk through them with an adult or trusted friend. Even wise people get angry (everyone does), but they know how to handle it.

REFLECT

How do you handle strong emotions? How can you cool down in moments of intense feelings?

# SEEKING GOD'S GUIDANCE

*Teach me your way, Lord, that I may rely on your faithfulness;*
*give me an undivided heart, that I may fear your name.*

**PSALM 86:11**

When you're going somewhere new, you enter the address into your phone, and the GPS guides your way there. That guidance is essential. Without it, you might make wrong turns and get lost. You don't just need that kind of guidance to get around—you need it to make big decisions, too. Maybe you can't decide if you should try out for the debate team. Or you need some direction on handling a conflict with a friend. Luckily, when we don't know our next steps, the Lord shows us the path to living a godly life.

King David admitted his need for God's guidance in Psalm 86. David wanted to learn God's way so that he would walk in truth. Because he obeyed God's Word, David could praise God in every aspect of his life. If we share the same desire to honor the Lord in our lives, we must seek God's truth.

One of the ways to receive guidance from the Lord is through His Word. The Bible tells us who God is. It reveals His love, power, and the relationship He wants to have with us. Not only can you find direction in Scripture, you can also pray to ask God for guidance in making the right decisions.

You can always ask for loving direction from our God. You don't need to make difficult decisions alone. God loves us and is there to guide us anytime we need.

REFLECT

What are some areas of your life right now where you could use a little guidance from God?

_____

_____

_____

# CHOOSING WHAT TO WATCH AND READ

Finally, brothers and sisters, whatever is true, whatever is noble,
whatever is right, whatever is pure, whatever is lovely,
whatever is admirable—if anything is excellent
or praiseworthy—think about such things.

**PHILIPPIANS 4:8**

When you're choosing what music, movies, and social media accounts to entertain yourself with, there are millions of options. Many of them are good. But there are an equal number of options that don't honor the Lord. It's important to make good choices when it comes to entertainment. The stories and ideas that we feed our minds with influence how we live our lives.

In the apostle Paul's letter to the Philippian church, he encouraged believers to think about things that are true, noble, right, pure, lovely, admirable, excellent, or praiseworthy. Notice that Paul's list doesn't include the words *popular* or *trendy*. This is because something can be popular without reflecting the values that are important in our lives.

When you choose your entertainment, Philippians 4:8 should be your guide. If something fits the list Paul gave, it's likely suitable for you. If it is not clear to you if a show you're interested in fits the qualities Paul described, try replacing each of the qualities with its opposite. For example, if a show highlights lies, it's not promoting truth.

Think carefully about what media you consume. Worship the Lord with the entertainment choices you make.

REFLECT

How do the music or movies you like influence the way you think and the words you use?

_____

_____

_____

# LOVING OTHERS

By this everyone will know that you are my disciples,
if you love one another.

JOHN 13:35

Sometimes it can feel like there are lots of complicated rules for how we, as Christians, are supposed to live. But the heart of loving Jesus is simple: love one another.

When Jesus explained this to His disciples in John 13, He was very close to His death. During this time, He asked His disciples to show a new level of commitment to one another because He knew they would really need each other's support. Having showed them what love looks like throughout His ministry, Jesus asked His disciples to follow His example. He still asks this of us today.

Every time you show love for someone, your classmates, teachers, parents, and family will understand your deep love for Jesus. Of course, you won't be perfect in loving everyone all the time, but each time you do something to show love, you show the world how great Jesus's love is.

Invite the Holy Spirit into your day and ask Him to show you ways to love other believers well. Ask Him to point out someone who needs encouragement. Perhaps you can text a friend and ask how you can pray for them. Don't settle for just being nice to someone today. Up your love for fellow believers by showing them the same love Jesus would.

REFLECT
How do you express love to others?

# ARGUING WITH OTHERS

*It is to one's honor to avoid strife, but every fool is quick to quarrel.*

PROVERBS 20:3

Arguing doesn't always involve fighting. When lawyers argue, they're doing their job, which is to defend their clients using facts. Calmly discussing an issue with others allows you to present your side of the story and learn a different perspective.

But most of your arguments probably don't look like calm discussions. They might be clashes with your siblings or conflicts with parents or coaches about what's expected of you. Every type of relationship will experience conflict. But when we fight, our tempers grow. We can become impatient and angry when we don't get our way.

The Bible says that it takes wisdom to put aside our desires to honor others' wishes and that it's good when we do so. Instead of fighting because you think you are right or because something didn't go your way, you can choose to listen to what others have to say. Avoiding strife doesn't mean you never experience conflict. Instead, when conflict happens, you can change your attitude by not getting defensive and by remembering to listen to other people's perspectives.

When your feelings are hurt or your pride is bruised, consider stepping away for a few moments to cool down before continuing the conversation. God's wisdom helps us avoid saying things in the heat of the moment that we will regret later.

REFLECT

When you argue, do you rationally present your opinion? How can you take steps to avoid arguing with those you are close to?

# BATTLING INSECURITY

You will keep in perfect peace those whose minds are steadfast,
because they trust in you.

**ISAIAH 26:3**

You might not realize it from looking, but everyone feels insecure sometimes. People might not feel confident about their looks, or they may doubt their talents. But while some insecurity is normal, a lot of insecurity can cause you to live in constant worry instead of living a life of peace.

Insecurity tempts us to think that our God-given gifts have little value. You may become insecure by putting your confidence in things outside of Christ. You might worry about what others think of you because you believe their opinion defines you. Or you place your identity in talents, like being naturally gifted in math. There's nothing wrong with recognizing other people's perceptions or acknowledging your strengths. But if you base your confidence on things that can change, your insecurity will grow. Someone will always be more likeable or smarter. Your worth isn't tied to how you measure up to others.

If you want consistent confidence, you must put your trust in God, who never changes. When you find yourself feeling shy or insecure, take a few quiet moments to remind yourself of the gifts God has given you. Remember that He wants you to share those gifts with the world. God offers you peace and support so that you can be strong and brave enough to share His love with others.

REFLECT

In what areas of your life do you struggle with insecurity?

_____

_____

_____

# BEING GENEROUS

When was the last time you were generous? Generosity means offering a gift or service when it is not expected. Maybe a friend was raising money for a mission trip, and you contributed some of your allowance to her fund. Or perhaps you heard about a cause that you wanted to support, so you hosted an event at school to raise awareness. A generous act can be big or small, and it doesn't always have to involve money—it only requires your heart.

When we are generous, we use the resources God has given us to help others. But using those resources doesn't mean we don't get to have them anymore—God supports our generosity by continuing to provide us with more resources. Your resources are like a pitcher of lemonade. If you use your lemonade to pour enough people's drinks, your pitcher will eventually be empty. But God will fill it up again so that you can share even more lemonade. When we are generous, God gives to us so that we can give to others.

Once you need to be filled again, the Lord promises you will receive refreshment yourself. Whether this blessing comes from Him or from someone else, you can trust God will take care of your every need. So, choose to be generous today. Give your time to help a sibling with homework. Build someone up with a word of encouragement. We honor the Lord when we mirror His generosity.

REFLECT

What is an example of something generous that someone did for you?

_____

_____

_____

# HOLDING EACH OTHER ACCOUNTABLE

*As iron sharpens iron, so one person sharpens another.*

PROVERBS 27:17

When it comes to friendship, the book of Proverbs says we are to sharpen each other spiritually. This is a metaphor based on the way that blacksmiths create swords. When the blacksmith strikes their metal with a hammer, both the sword and the iron are sharpened. They mutually make each other stronger. We mimic this process in our friendships when we hold each other accountable for our actions.

In these types of friendships, you willingly give friends access to your heart, sharing weaknesses and mistakes with them in confidence. These friends can ask tough questions about your discipline, temptation, and sin. Knowing that they love you and will hold you accountable to your actions pushes you to make good decisions. Though accountability sometimes involves correcting friends, it is a gift to belong to a community of other believers.

Friends like these cheer you on when you obey the Lord and lovingly point out your mistakes so that you can grow. When you are discouraged, they pray for you. If you need a reminder of truth, they send you verses to look up and study. These friends don't ask you to be perfect, but they do push you to seek Jesus passionately.

If you want to continue to grow in your faith and find yourself discouraged, pray for the Lord to give you a friend who will hold you accountable. When you find someone to encourage you as you support them, you can't help but grow closer to Christ.

REFLECT

What does accountability mean to you? Is there someone in your life who might help you and hold you accountable?

---

---

---

# ASKING FOR WISDOM

*If any of you lacks wisdom, you should ask God, who gives generously to all without finding fault, and it will be given to you.*

**JAMES 1:5**

Wisdom helps you combine your love for God with the facts about a situation. It guides you to consider all sides of a question and then leads you to do what's biblically right. For instance, maybe you don't know how to handle a conflict with your friends. God's wisdom handles hard situations with biblical truth instead of personal desires, helping you become a peacemaker in a stressful situation.

In the New Testament, James wrote a letter of encouragement to believers. One of the first things he talked about in this letter was experiencing hard times or temptations. James reminded us that when we lack spiritual understanding, we should always ask God for wisdom. God promises to give wisdom to anyone who asks for it. You don't ever need to be embarrassed about needing help.

Ultimately, the Lord gives us wisdom for our benefit. It keeps us from paying the consequences for potential mistakes. The next time you face a situation that you don't know how to handle, don't feel like you have to figure it out on your own. The Lord promises to give us wisdom, so ask for it.

**REFLECT**

When's the last time you asked God for wisdom? How did it help you make the right decision in a situation?

# SERVING OTHERS

When you hear the word *service*, you might think of a server bring-
ing food to your table at a restaurant. But service means something
different for believers. As Christ's followers, our lives are not about
us. We are called to use our freedom to serve others.

When Paul wrote the church in Galatia, he reminded believers
to use their freedom wisely. Some of the members of the church
knew that Christ had set them free from their sins, but they saw this
freedom as an invitation to do whatever they wanted. Instead of
excusing their sinful behaviors, Paul called on them to serve others
out of humility and love. He challenged them to live like Jesus.

Christ gave up the comfort of Heaven to come to Earth. Though
He of all people deserves to be praised and served, even Jesus
"did not come to be served, but to serve" (Mark 10:45). One of the
greatest ways that you can show God's goodness is by following
Christ's example and putting the needs of others above your own
needs or desires.

There are many small acts of service that you can do for others.
Your mom would probably love help with the laundry. An elderly
neighbor might need someone to walk her dog. A friend might
need help with homework in a subject that comes easily to you.
Christ set us free to love Him and to love others. We can follow
His lead every day.

REFLECT

How does it make you feel when someone puts your wants before their own?

# BEING A PEACEMAKER

*Blessed are the peacemakers,*
*for they will be called children of God.*

MATTHEW 5:9

Have you ever been caught in the middle of a fight? It's no fun to be caught between friends who are arguing. In these moments, you have the choice to be either a peacemaker or a peacekeeper. While peacekeeping and peacemaking sound like they have the same goal, they involve different approaches and use different definitions for peace.

If you are a peacekeeper, you do whatever it takes to keep things quiet and calm. You might try to avoid conflict or squash an argument. This passive approach is about trying to help everyone just get along. Although peacekeeping might keep things calm in the moment, it doesn't help anyone solve their problems or communicate their needs.

On the other hand, peacemaking helps others actively resolve their problems. Instead of telling others what they want to hear, peacemakers step into conflict to shed light on everyone's viewpoint. Being a peacemaker isn't always comfortable, but it restores unity during moments of conflict.

If friends begin to argue, help them understand each other's perspectives. Or if you find yourself in a fight, choose to make peace by compromising and talking through the issue. If we create peace, we will be known as children of the ultimate peacemaker: Jesus.

REFLECT

What is your definition of peace? How can you be a peacemaker instead of a peacekeeper?

# PLANNING WISELY

In their hearts humans plan their course,
but the Lord establishes their steps.

**PROVERBS 16:9**

When was the last time your plans didn't work out? Maybe your friends backed out of a party you'd organized, or you didn't make the team after months of practice. Unfortunately, life doesn't always go according to plan. That's why it is important to plan and to learn to yield to God's plans.

Taking the time to plan is a sign of responsibility. Planning gives you a strategy to follow and helps you handle unexpected changes. If you want to grow as an athlete, you need to plan to spend more time in the gym. If you want to make straight As, you have to plan time to study.

But even plans you worked really hard on might not turn out. When something doesn't go how you planned, remember, as Proverbs tells us, that God establishes your steps. His plans won't always line up with yours, but you can trust Him. God knows why you didn't make the basketball team and how your family will survive your parents' divorce. The Lord has a full picture of your life, while you only have a limited view of your circumstances.

When situations are out of your control, you can choose to get frustrated or you can learn to be flexible. It is important to keep making plans. But be ready to adapt to the changes God is making and grow in your trust in Him. As a result, you will deepen your dependence on Him and be ready for the next time plans change.

REFLECT
How has planning helped you in the past? Who in your life can help you trust God's plan when you feel disappointed or confused?

# WORKING TOGETHER

*Two are better than one, because
they have a good return for their labor.*
ECCLESIASTES 4:9

Imagine what the world would look like if we never worked with others. Playing most sports would be impossible. Symphonies would become solos. We would feel lonely at home, school, church, and work. Luckily, God did not intend for us to live life alone.

In the Old Testament, King Solomon was known for his wisdom, a gift he was granted by God. In Ecclesiastes, he wrote about these things, noting that living life alone adds to our hardships. Solomon decided that we are better when we are together.

There are many benefits to working in a team setting. Having teammates on a project lightens the load and stress of the task you are working on, making it easier for everyone to do their best work and produce a better result.

Not only does working with teammates help you accomplish more, but you also grow when you learn from those who are different from you. Someone might have a skill you don't have, adding to the project in a way you wouldn't have considered. And you have gifts that others can benefit from. Unity comes from understanding that every person has unique talents, strengths, and weaknesses.

The next time you find yourself working with a team, use the opportunity to celebrate the gifts of those around you and learn from those who are different from you.

REFLECT

When did you accomplish more with a team than you could have by yourself?

# STRUGGLING WITH DEPRESSION

*Why, my soul, are you downcast? Why so disturbed*
*with me? Put your hope in God, for I will yet praise Him,*
*my Savior and my God.*

PSALM 42:11

Depression is one of the most overwhelming emotions. It zaps our energy, motivation, and hope, making our souls incredibly downcast.

The writer of Psalm 42 felt depressed. The stressful circumstances around him made him feel anxious and worried. He knew where his pain was coming from, but he also knew where to put his hope.

When you start to experience despair, ask yourself: why is my soul hurting? There are many reasons why we experience sadness. Once you know the root of your depression, you can better address your next steps to overcome it.

A natural step after recognizing the cause of your sadness is to place your hope in God. When you turn to God, you can find strength in His love and remember that your circumstances are temporary. God is in control!

Trusting Jesus when you feel depressed doesn't change your circumstances, but it anchors you to the One who does not change. Christ's faithfulness can help guide and support you to find hope again.

Sometimes when you are depressed, you need more than spiritual hope. If you turn to God for help but still struggle with depression, talk to a trusted adult about other kinds of help that might be available, too.

REFLECT
What characteristics of God reassure you when you are feeling your worst?

_____

_____

_____

# OBEYING THE LORD

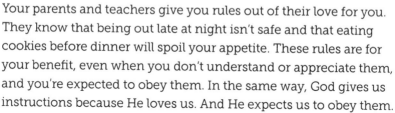

*We know that we have come to know Him
if we keep His commands.*

**1 JOHN 2:3**

Your parents and teachers give you rules out of their love for you. They know that being out late at night isn't safe and that eating cookies before dinner will spoil your appetite. These rules are for your benefit, even when you don't understand or appreciate them, and you're expected to obey them. In the same way, God gives us instructions because He loves us. And He expects us to obey them.

Throughout the Bible, we see examples of the commands that God gives His people. The Lord asks us to love Him with all of our hearts, to obey our parents, and to show His love to others. These aren't suggestions or helpful hints; they are rules to follow. Though these rules might seem designed to restrict our fun, it's actually quite the opposite. The Lord sees every consequence of our actions and doesn't want us to bring unnecessary harm or sin into our lives. Not only does obedience protect our hearts; it also shows our love for Christ. Only those who trust God obey His commands.

If you are angry, it might feel good to retaliate against a friend, but God knows the harm your anger might inflict on a friendship. When you disrespect your parents, the Lord knows the results of not honoring them. Instead of trying to do things your way, submit to the Lord. There will be less pain, fewer consequences, and more joy when you decide to obey God.

**REFLECT**
When is obeying God challenging for you?

_____

_____

_____

# LIVING COMPASSIONATELY

*Be kind and compassionate to one another, forgiving each other, just as in Christ God forgave you.*

**EPHESIANS 4:32**

When you see others feeling sad or hurt, it's natural to want to stop their pain. If a friend is crying in the locker room, you might give her a hug, offer to listen to her problems, and distract her with humor. Or you might tell a classmate whose parents are going through a divorce about the love of Jesus. Helping others when they hurt, without caring whether they'll pay us back, is the definition of compassion.

Christ taught us what compassion is when He died on the Cross. Jesus saw the way sin impacts our lives—it affects our hearts, our world, and our relationship with Him. Instead of leaving us in pain, He had sympathy for us. He left the comforts of Heaven and died to alleviate our spiritual suffering. This is the true definition of compassion.

Christ's example invites us to share similar sympathy for others. You might show compassion through something small, like paying for somebody's lunch when they forget their money at home. Or you might try to help in a big way, like raising money each month to support a charity you're passionate about. Our sympathy for others' suffering reflects the Lord's great kindness to us. Compassion challenges us to step up and meet the needs of those around us.

REFLECT

When has someone's compassion helped you through a situation?

# TRUSTING OTHERS

And let us consider how we may spur one another on
toward love and good deeds, not giving up meeting together,
as some are in the habit of doing, but encouraging one another—
and all the more as you see the Day approaching.

**HEBREWS 10:24–25**

When was the last time someone disappointed you? Maybe a friend
canceled plans at the last second, or a parent didn't hold up their
end of a bargain. The people you rely on will let you down at some
point—that's true for everyone. When this happens, it's natural to
pull away in frustration or disappointment. But if you aren't careful,
mistrust might prevent you from living a life of love.

One of the greatest joys and comforts in life comes from leaning
on one another. Our friends celebrate the joyful things in our lives
and mourn with us in our sadness. Our community spurs us on
toward love and good deeds. We grow in our relationship with the
Lord while we grow closer to others.

We need family members, teachers, and friends to support us
during good times and bad. But living life in fellowship with others
is messy. We are all imperfect people. This reality means others
will unintentionally hurt us and need our forgiveness. So, we must
learn how to love, trust, and forgive others and hope that they will
do the same for us.

God designed our lives to be filled with other people who will help
us grow closer to Him. Don't let the fear of being hurt or let down
outweigh the benefits of community. Choose to lean on trustworthy
people and forgive the ones you love when they make mistakes.

REFLECT
What does trust mean to you?

_____

_____

_____

# BEING HONEST

*The Lord detests lying lips,*
*but He delights in people who are trustworthy.*

**PROVERBS 12:22**

God is the God of truth. When you choose to tell the truth, you reflect the Lord's character and honor Him through your honesty. However, though everyone knows honesty is the best policy, we don't always choose to tell the truth.

Sometimes, you might mistakenly believe that lying will help you. When you want to get out of trouble, telling a lie can allow you to temporarily escape the consequences. Or maybe you tell white lies when you're telling real stories because you want to make your stories funnier or more exciting. In those cases, lying might bring short-term relief. But it hurts you in the long run.

When someone tells a lie, it shows a lot about their heart. We use lies when we are afraid or when we know we've made a mistake and don't want people to know. Even if no one ever finds out, you are left with the knowledge that you told a lie. And if the truth is revealed, you usually end up in more trouble than you would have been in if you had told the truth in the first place.

The Bible is clear about God's thoughts on dishonesty. He cannot stand when our speech is full of deceit. The next time you have the opportunity to be dishonest, remember God delights in those who tell the truth.

REFLECT
Think of a time you told a lie. How did lying cost you more in the long run than telling the truth would have?

# SETTING GOALS

The plans of the diligent lead to profit
as surely as haste leads to poverty.
PROVERBS 21:5

Goals challenge us to grow physically, emotionally, and spiritually. If you're a cross-country runner, you might set the goal of breaking your own record for a three-mile run. If you want to use your time wisely after school, you might work on the goal of having all your homework done by dinnertime. Goals serve as a road map, helping us realize where we are, where we want to be, and how we plan on getting there. They help us live our lives wisely.

Proverbs tells us that planning ways to reach our goals benefits us. And when we rush into something without planning, we often don't get the results we want. You might have high hopes, but if you don't discipline yourself to work toward your goal, you will never accomplish it. Therefore, you must plan out how you will reach your goals.

Planning helps you take practical steps toward your goals. You can conquer tasks when you know exactly what they require. Choose goals you can realistically achieve. Good goals challenge you to grow but aren't so big that they'll discourage you from moving forward. Ultimately, setting goals honors the Lord in your life. It shows that you want to manage His gifts and blessings wisely.

So, the next time you accomplish a goal, celebrate. You worked hard to grow in that area of life. After reflecting on what you learned, repeat the process in another area of your life.

REFLECT

When was the last time you set a goal for yourself? How did planning out specific steps help you accomplish what you wanted?

_____

_____

_____

# ASKING GOD FOR HELP

*Let us then approach God's throne of grace with confidence,
so that we may receive mercy and find grace
to help us in our time of need.*

**HEBREWS 4:16**

When you don't understand something in class, you raise your hand to get your teacher's help. And your teacher is probably happy to help. A good teacher would rather you come to them for clarification than try to figure everything out on your own. God also wants us to go to Him when we need answers to life's questions. He doesn't think we should figure it out on our own; He wants to give us help.

The Lord loves when we ask Him about anything, from important issues to the seemingly insignificant areas of our lives. When you ask for help, it shows you trust that your Creator can keep providing for you. When you ask for help avoiding a temptation or coping with the death of a loved one, you admit that you don't have all the answers. When you don't know what to do, it's okay; you have a God who does.

The Lord wants us to turn to Him with every small or large request. He can help us with everything we experience. God promises to provide a way out of temptation. If your faith is running low, He can give you a double dose. Hebrews 4:16 reminds you that you can confidently ask for grace and mercy any time you need it.

Just like a loving teacher, God doesn't want you to try to figure out life on your own. The next time you are in a time of need, go directly to God. He's waiting for you to turn to Him.

REFLECT

When was a time you turned to God for help? How did you receive comfort and direction from His Word?

_____

_____

_____

# FINDING PEACE

Let the peace of Christ rule in your hearts,
since as members of one body you were called to peace.

COLOSSIANS 3:15

Conflict happens. You may have argued with siblings or experienced drama with friends. And you've probably felt disappointed when things didn't go the way you expected them to or felt angry or jealous when you thought you weren't being treated fairly. With all this noise and chaos going on around you, it can be hard to find a way to quiet your soul. The answer to all this conflict is God's peace.

When Paul reminded the Colossian church about God's peace, he said they must let it rule their hearts. If our hearts and minds are a battlefield, we must let God's peace win the battle. We decide how we react to conflict and anxiety. Someone filled with God's peace doesn't fear a math test or get anxious about tryouts. They know God has a plan, regardless of the outcome. Life's curveballs don't discourage them.

You can find peace no matter what is happening in your life because you know that God loves you, and you can trust that He is in control. The Lord's love can quiet your heart when anxieties swirl within you. His peace is there whenever you need it. God's peace can make you feel calm when you are upset or help you find kind, helpful words when someone makes you angry.

If you want peace in your heart, take time to notice when your fear feels stronger than your faith. Let peace reign in your heart by praying to the Lord about your anxiety and worry.

REFLECT
What makes you feel worried or angry? What makes you feel peaceful?

# ENCOURAGING OTHERS

Gracious words are a honeycomb,
sweet to the soul and healing to the bones.

**PROVERBS 16:24**

When was the last time someone said something encouraging to you? Maybe you had a rough day, and someone complimented your outfit to boost your confidence. Or perhaps a friend saw you were discouraged and reminded you of how awesome you are. Life is full of challenges that can bring you down. But a gracious word from someone can instantly lift the spirit.

Receiving encouragement does wonders for our hearts. It gives us hope and pushes us to keep going. Encouragement reminds us that we are seen, loved, and valued. King Solomon even compared pleasant words to the sweetness of honey, the purest form of sugar available during biblical times.

Other people's words have great power in your life. And you can use encouragement as a way to support those around you, too. You have the power to remind a friend of her unique beauty when she is feeling shy or insecure. If your sister is trying to be kinder to others, you can let her know that you've seen a difference in her behavior. Encouragement is a powerful tool that we can use to strengthen those around us. It builds up the people we love.

Saying a kind word to someone costs you nothing but benefits those who hear it. Use encouragement as a way to inspire your friends and family today.

REFLECT

When was the last time someone told you something sweet that refreshed your heart? Is there anyone in your life who could use a little extra encouragement?

_____

_____

_____

# KEEPING SECRETS

A gossip betrays a confidence,
but a trustworthy person keeps a secret.
PROVERBS 11:13

When a friend reveals the name of their crush or a problem they are struggling with, they expect you to keep this information private. If they wanted others to know, they could have shared it at the lunch table or told everyone on the bus. Instead, they came to you quietly, asking you to keep their secret in confidence.

It is important for all of us to have people we can speak to about our deepest worries and private thoughts. And if someone has spoken to you about their worries, it is equally important to keep their secrets to yourself. Other people's secrets are not your stories to share. Of course, there are specific instances where you might need to tell a trusted adult, like if a friend mentions she's hurting herself, hurting others, or being hurt by others. Otherwise, you must honor your friend's wishes for privacy and confidence.

If you've ever had a friend share your secret, you know how incredibly hurtful their betrayal felt. Breaking someone's trust creates pain.

Honor your friends by not spilling the beans. Keeping their secret shows you value them as friends and can handle the good, the bad, and the messy parts of their lives. If someone provides some details about their life in confidence, cherish them by tucking that story away in your heart. Honor the Lord by honoring your word to keep others' secrets.

REFLECT
When was the last time you told someone a secret? How did their response affect your friendship?

_____

_____

_____

# WATCHING WHAT YOU SAY

*Do not let any unwholesome talk come out of your mouths,*
*but only what is helpful for building others up according*
*to their needs, that it may benefit those who listen.*

**EPHESIANS 4:29**

Gossiping often traps you into speaking ill of someone behind their back. It can get you in trouble, and saying cruel things ultimately distances you from Christ's command to love your neighbor.

The Bible teaches us that our words are the overflow of our hearts (Matthew 12:34). If you say things that are unwholesome or unkind, you need to look at what is in your heart. If we fail to love Christ deep in our hearts, our words will reflect this.

But when Christ is the treasure of your heart, you naturally find yourself building others up. Whether you cheer your friends on to seek the best for their lives or offer a kind word of encouragement to a classmate, God's love spills over into your everyday conversations. This overflow is contagious, uplifting, and glorifying to the Lord.

The Holy Spirit helps us filter what we think and, as a result, what we say. If sharing God's love through your words is hard, don't fix the fruit, check the root. Why do you feel pressured to use certain words or speak a certain way? Confess your mistakes to the Lord and apologize to anyone you might have hurt with your words. Then, remind yourself of the Lord's goodness. Your speech will soon follow your heart.

REFLECT
Have you ever said something that got you in trouble or hurt someone's feelings?

_____

_____

_____

# FINDING STRENGTH IN GOD

*Even youths grow tired and weary, and young men stumble and fall; but those who hope in the Lord will renew their strength. They will soar on wings like eagles; they will run and not grow weary, they will walk and not be faint.*

ISAIAH 40:30–31

We all know what it feels like to be tired. You might have felt tired after a long week at school or after working out hard at cheerleading practice. But your physical body isn't the only thing that can become tired. Our hearts and minds can grow weary, too. When you find yourself needing rest, the Lord offers support.

The Bible reminds us that, at some point in time, everyone will grow weak and need God's strength. You may feel great pain and sorrow after the death of a loved one. Or you might be failing a class even though you are studying incredibly hard. God is not surprised that you are tired when heavy things are happening in your life. He loves you enough to give you what you need.

When life doesn't seem to go your way, you must rely on the Lord. He gives us strength when we are at our weakest. He gives us hope when we are discouraged. God will provide you with more power, more rest, and more energy than any nap ever could. Instead of navigating life alone, ask the Lord for help. Spend some time reading your favorite Bible verses or take an extra few minutes to pray. Share your feelings and frustrations, and ask God to strengthen you. He promises to help you soar through these situations with the power of His hope.

REFLECT

Has there been a time in your life when you felt emotionally tired or discouraged?

# LIVING OUT YOUR FAITH

*In the same way, faith by itself,*
*if it is not accompanied by action, is dead.*

**JAMES 2:17**

Have you ever known someone whose words didn't match up with their actions? Maybe a friend promised to return your favorite sweater but kept forgetting to bring it to school day after day. Or your parents promised to take you on a camping trip if you got a good report card, yet every time you ask about it, they push the date back several weekends. You can gauge someone's intentions by how their words match their actions. Likewise, if you say you believe in Jesus, you have to show your faith through actions that spread God's love.

In the Bible, the apostle James described it this way: Imagine someone declares they love Jesus, but then doesn't help their friend who needs food. You could say that they have faith, but they aren't acting on it. The Lord tells us to love our neighbor, but withholding food from someone who is starving is not loving behavior. Our faith in Jesus should inspire us to act with joy, patience, kindness, and humility every day, because our actions mirror the Word of God that is deep in our hearts.

The way you live should be a window into the faith you have in Christ. How do your actions demonstrate your trust in Jesus? If others can tell you follow Christ by the way you love others, you have a living faith. If you need some help in this area, ask the Lord to help you grow. He will remind you of His goodness when you need it.

REFLECT

What has your faith in God taught you about how to treat others?

_____

_____

_____

# MAKING NEW FRIENDS

*Love does no harm to a neighbor.*
**ROMANS 13:10**

When a group of friends doesn't invite others into their circle, that group becomes a clique. For the people inside of this clique, it feels like they're just hanging out with familiar friends. But when you are on the outside, it's lonely. It is important to always make new friends so you can continue sharing God's love with the people around you.

God invites us to love everyone because He loves everyone. When we don't extend friendship or kindness to our neighbor, we fail to obey the Lord.

If you don't challenge yourself to get outside of your comfort zone, you rob friendship from those who need it most. If you only chat with your friends in class, the lonely girl sitting next to you won't feel welcome to join the conversation. There is no harm in inviting her to sit with your friends at lunch. It costs nothing to share love, and it gives others the joy of feeling seen.

Plus, when you aren't open to new friends, you miss out on new, interesting friendships. Though people gravitate toward others with similar interests, don't let this limit you to only making friends who like the same stuff you do. You will never learn new things if you don't open up your friend selection.

You don't have to be best friends with everyone you meet. However, love never does anyone harm. Choose to make a new friend by giving someone your attention and affection.

REFLECT
Do you make new friends often? If so, how does it feel? If not, what keeps you from reaching out to new people?

# VALUING YOUR SIBLINGS

*If it is possible, as far as it depends on you,*
*live at peace with everyone.*

ROMANS 12:18

Everyone fights with their brothers and sisters. If you're like most people, you probably argue over small things, like who gets the last waffle. But it can still feel frustrating.

The Bible is full of stories about siblings who fought, including the very first pair of brothers, Cain and Abel. After years of separation, Moses was reunited with his siblings, but the three of them clashed often. Even Jesus's siblings ridiculed Him early on in His ministry. Comparisons and competition quickly start family fights. But God asks that you live in peace with everyone, including your siblings.

Whether you want control of the TV remote or have more serious problems, fights with siblings are usually rooted in selfishness. You may be placing your wants and desires before their needs. But this prevents you from being the peacemaker that God asks us all to be.

Your siblings are a unique gift. They are the only ones who can relate to your family's circumstances, and they know you best. So, try your hardest to interact with them peacefully, out of love for them and the Lord. Instead of fighting to get your way, put them first. It's not always easy or fun to serve your siblings, but in doing so, you put God's love into action.

REFLECT

Why do you and your siblings fight? What is something kind that you could do for a sibling to show how much you care?

_____

_____

_____

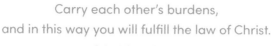

*Carry each other's burdens,
and in this way you will fulfill the law of Christ.*

GALATIANS 6:2

Have you ever tried to move a piece of furniture by yourself? If so, you know how much easier it was when someone came along to pick up the other side. Though it is possible to move heavy objects alone, help from others makes it easier. In the same way, God calls on us all to help others carry their emotional and spiritual burdens. You can alleviate the weight of people's pain by offering to support them.

One of the easiest ways you can help others is by meeting their physical needs. Maybe a friend struggles to open her locker every morning. Making an effort to help her before class starts each day would reduce the amount of stress and anxiety she faces. It's a small way to show her you care.

Helping a friend with emotional burdens, like a parent's job loss or a loved one's cancer diagnosis, is a little more complicated. Sometimes, a friend in a rough situation needs emotional support. Lend a listening ear, or treat them to a night of fun.

When you carry someone else's burdens, you share the love of Jesus. After all, that's what Jesus did for us. He paid the price for our sins when we could not help ourselves. Helping out is a simple way to share God's love with a friend or family member.

REFLECT
When did someone help you through a hard situation?

_____

_____

_____

# CONFESSING AND REPENTING OF SIN

*Whoever conceals their sins does not prosper, but the one who confesses and renounces them finds mercy.*

**PROVERBS 28:13**

It's natural to want to hide your mistakes. You might not want your parents to know you broke a window, or your friend to know that you accidentally shared their secret. But the Bible is clear: hiding a sin is not to our benefit. When we conceal our sins instead of asking for forgiveness, our spirits become heavy.

Confession means telling the Lord about your sins. There are a lot of different ways to confess. You might confess in prayer or tell a friend about your sins. The important thing is that you admit your guilt to God.

The Lord already knows your sin. But admitting your wrongdoing shows that you acknowledge your mistake. By revealing sin instead of hiding it, you can move on through repentance—the process of changing your heart, mind, and direction. Repentance pushes you to pursue Christ instead of continuing to sin.

Though you must turn to the Lord for confession and repentance, you don't have to go through this process alone. First, confess your guilt to the Lord. Then, consider telling a trusted adult or friend. They can encourage you and pray for you to find victory in Christ.

The Lord promises to forgive us and purify us if we confess our wrongdoing to Him. Instead of hiding sin, admit and repent of your wrongdoing. You will experience God's mercy and forgiveness as a result.

REFLECT

What sins do you need to confess to the Lord? How can you turn to the Lord in repentance instead of repeating the same mistakes again?

_____

_____

_____

# CELEBRATING OUR FREEDOM

*It is for freedom that Christ has set us free. Stand firm, then, and do not let yourselves be burdened again by a yoke of slavery.*

GALATIANS 5:1

The Fourth of July is more than a fun time for fireworks and barbecues; it's a day to celebrate our freedom. As Americans, we have the liberty to think about what we want, believe what we want, and say the things we want. These freedoms are available to us because people sacrificed their lives to defend the ideals of our country. Our spiritual freedom also comes through sacrifice— Christ's death on the Cross.

Godly freedom is different from political freedom. Godly freedom means that Christ sets us free from sin. This is good news for anyone who feels trapped into making the same mistakes. Maybe it seems impossible to break the habit of gossip. But because of God's freedom, your mouth does not have control over you. Or perhaps it is hard for you to consider the needs of others when there is something that you want badly. But because of God's freedom, your desires do not have power over you. Instead of walking in sin, you can follow our Savior's freedom.

You can either let your sin influence your heart and actions, or you can give control of your life to Jesus. But you cannot do both. Christ died to set you free from sin so you could walk rightly with Him instead of choosing wrongdoing. Choose to lay down the pain of your mistakes for the joy of a life full of godly freedom.

REFLECT

What areas of your life do you want to change, but you feel stuck or trapped in? How can you remind yourself of the spiritual freedom given to you in Christ?

# WEARING THE ARMOR OF GOD

*Finally, be strong in the Lord and in His mighty power.*
*Put on the full armor of God, so that you can*
*take your stand against the devil's schemes.*

EPHESIANS 6:10–11

Most of us think of armor as something that protects soldiers in battle. But while you might not be in a physical war, the Bible says we are in a spiritual battle against sin and Satan. Luckily, God gave us the armor we need to best fight our enemy.

Paul described the armor of God in his letter to the Ephesians—a belt of truth, a breastplate of righteousness, and shoes of peace. These pieces of armor protect us from Satan's lies, anxieties, and worries. We also have a shield of faith and the helmet of salvation, which keeps our minds fixed on God's love and forgiveness.

The Lord also gives us one weapon to fight with: the sword of the Spirit. God's Word is our best attack against hurt and lies. The Bible uproots lies and replaces them with the truth. Nothing can defeat Satan quicker than using Scripture to protect our hearts and minds.

Though it's hard to imagine that you're in a spiritual battle, you need to fight against the forces in the world that bring hate, anger, and dishonesty. Because you put on the armor of God, you receive the strength of the Lord to keep fighting. While getting ready every morning, choose to put on the armor of God before any other accessory.

REFLECT

What piece of armor do you need the most right now? How has Scripture helped you fight against temptation?

# INCLUDING OTHERS

We love because He first loved us.

1 JOHN 4:19

Have you ever felt excluded? If so, you know it's not fun to feel disconnected from others. We believers must love everyone, just as God first loved us.

Jesus left the comfort of Heaven to die on the Cross for us. This choice to lovingly sacrifice Himself makes His forgiveness available for everyone. No one is excluded from God's grace. Our actions should mimic the way He first loved us: constantly, in action, and including everyone.

In the New Testament, Paul gave the perfect definition of how to love others like Christ. 1 Corinthians 13:4–8 says: "Love is patient, love is kind. It does not envy, it does not boast, it is not proud. It does not dishonor others, it is not self-seeking, it is not easily angered, it keeps no record of wrongs. Love does not delight in evil but rejoices with the truth. It always protects, always trusts, always hopes, always perseveres. Love never fails."

These qualities are how you know if you are loving others the way you should. You don't get the chance to love others if you don't include them. God's love is an open-ended invitation that you can pass along to others. Share the hope and love of Jesus by making someone feel seen and included today. Love others like Christ first loved you by giving generously and by showing your love through actions.

REFLECT

What are some ways Christ has shown love to you? How can you share the Lord's love by including someone today?

# LOVING OTHERS LIKE JESUS

*This is love: not that we loved God, but that He loved us and sent His Son as an atoning sacrifice for our sins. Dear friends, since God so loved us, we also ought to love one another.*

1 JOHN 4:10–11

Trying to understand the Lord's love for us is like trying to calculate how much water is in the ocean. It's nearly impossible! Though it's hard to wrap your mind around the extent of God's love, every aspect of your life should overflow with gratitude for it.

John knew God's love incredibly well. He was one of Jesus's closest disciples. When he tried to encourage the early church, John often focused on the power of God's love. In 1 John 4, John even says God *is* love. Every aspect of the Lord is loving, kind, and gracious. He doesn't withhold this love from anyone; He gives it freely to all. We can mirror this by loving others with this same love.

Love doesn't always come naturally. It is hard to like people who make fun of you or say mean things. Though it's easier to show love to those who treat you kindly, God's love invites you to love those who are rude as much as those who are kind. Mean or friendly, tall or short, stranger or friend, you should not treat anyone differently. As Christ's follower, you must love everyone as Jesus loves us all.

None of us have earned God's love. He gives it to us freely. Therefore, none of us get to choose who we show God's love to. Wherever you go today, love everyone.

REFLECT
Name some ways God has demonstrated His love for you. How has your life reflected this type of powerful love for others?

# GROWING UP GRACEFULLY

Teach us to number our days,
that we may gain a heart of wisdom.

**PSALM 90:12**

*I can't wait until* _____ *!* Whether you are
dreaming about the day when you start high school, get your
driver's license, or begin college, there are so many fun mile-
stones to reach as you grow up. But if you aren't careful, you can
wish your days away, longing for tomorrow. To gracefully grow
up into the person God calls you to be, you must use your days
wisely. Or, as Scripture puts it, you need to number your days.

This tension between living significantly and living selfishly is
what the prayer of Moses in Psalm 90 addresses. Moses prayed for
God to teach us to number our days. On our own, we don't naturally choose to live intentionally for the Lord. This kind of graceful
and responsible living only comes about when we realize that
nothing in the future is a guarantee. When we are young, it seems
like we have the rest of our lives to start living for the Lord. But it is
not wise to waste your youth.

You grow up gracefully when you commit to using your time to
love Jesus and others. As Paul encouraged the Ephesian church,
"Be very careful, then, how you live—not as unwise but as wise,
making the most of every opportunity, because the days are evil"
(Ephesians 5:15–17). Ask the Lord to give you a heart of wisdom so
that you may live your days for Him.

REFLECT

What are some opportunities that you want to make the most of in your life?

_____

_____

_____

# INDEX OF SCRIPTURES

# INDEX OF TOPICS

# ABOUT THE AUTHOR

 **Megan Gover** is the president of Minted Truth, an online Bible study resource for teen girls around the world. She and her team have led thousands of teen girls to know Christ on a deeper level through Bible studies and resources available on their free Minted Truth app. In addition, she regularly writes and speaks at girls' conferences and local churches. Megan's desire is for teen girls to know their Bibles better and to know their Savior deeper. Whether she's meeting with teen girls at a local coffee shop or dreaming up a new Bible study, she prays this generation knows and loves the Lord.

When not discipling and teaching middle school and high school girls, Megan spends time with friends and family at the lake. She especially enjoys cuddling with her goldendoodle pup while at home in North Texas.

CPSIA information can be obtained
at www.ICGtesting.com
Printed in the USA
JSHW031441030921
18412JS00010B/79

9 781647 396954